Growing Up
in an
Amish-Jewish Cult

Book One
Delusion

Patricia Hochstetler

Growing Up
in an
Amish-Jewish Cult

Book One
Delusion

BAKER TRITTIN PRESS
Winona Lake, Indiana

Growing Up in an Amish-Jewish Cult / Book One, Delusion
By Patricia Hochstetler

Printed in the United States of America
Cover Design: Paul S. Trittin
Back Cover Photos: Mike Albin
Published by Baker Trittin Press
P.O. Box 277
Winona Lake, Indiana 46590

To order additional copies please call (888) 741-4386
or email info@btconcepts.com
http://www.bakertrittinpress.com

Publishers Cataloging-Publication Data
Patricia Hochstetler, 1948-
        Growing Up in an Amish-Jewish Cult/ Book One, Delusion
        Patricia Hochstetler - Winona Lake, Indiana
        Baker Trittin Press, 2007

                p.   cm.

Library of Congress Control Number: 200792549
ISBN 10: 0-9787316-4-6
ISBN 13: 978-0-9787316-4-9
        1. Autobiography 2. Religious 3. Christian
        I. Title   II. Growing Up in an Amish-Jewish Cult /
        Book One, Delusion
BIO18000

Second Printing

Acknowledgements

The following individuals have played critical roles in the creation of this book and the two books which follow. I thank each one for the part they have played.

The late Dr. John Cooper, my Writer's Digest Instructor, gave me direction and encouraged me to keep writing and attend college. The late Ken Anderson and Mrs. Anderson took me under their wings, guided and helped me. Cindi Randolph and Sherri Hess along with Jay Bentson helped with transcribing my many taped interviews. The Bethel College professors and writing club members, helped me with English, computers, writing, editing and encouragement, and also the members of the Ft. Wayne area Christian Writer's Club.

I must also aknowledge all of the Lael Colony members who shared their experiences with me and my mom who answered so many of my questions,

None of this book could have been written without the patience and support of my husband, Ezra, my children and grandchildren, and my friends and church family.

My editor, Dr. Marvin G. Baker, and publication advisor, Paul Trittin, offered continuous encouragement and were outstanding in their dedication to bring the dangers of cults to the attention of the public.

Mostly, I must thank Jesus Christ my Lord, who with love, mercy, and grace, spared my life and delivered me from despair.

Table of Contents

Preface

Cults! Large or small, mainstream or obscure, exotic or simple - they are still Cults! Theological subtleties twist truth into contorted reflections impossible to discern. Cults!

Charismatic personalities persuade multitudes to follow the imaginings of deceiving minds. Cults! Innocent children, victims all, become stranded in the quagmire of misguided beliefs and dangle over an abyss of fear and desperation. Cults!

Delusion is the story of one child, Patricia Hochstetler, caught in the trap of parental good intentions. Between the ages of four and six she was snatched from the warmth of *Jesus Loves Me* and thrust into a world that was cold and barren. Her plaintive question, "Why can't I play with a doll?" went unanswered.

She wanted to please God and her parents, but the harder she tried the more desperate and confused she became. "Why is my aunt hiding out in the woods? Why did my cousin get taken out and dumped? Why is my father acting so strange? What can I do to be sure I'm going to heaven?" The unspoken questions, even of a child, could never be answered for no one dared question the rules.

The author reminds us that no one decides to join a *cult*. Parents set out to find truth, to draw closer to God. In their wayward search their children become scarred, sometimes eternally scarred. Confusion reigns because the rules change for no apparent reason. If it was good yesterday, why is it bad today? Parents who are incapable of discerning what is truth and blindly accept the word of a

9

leader are dangerously close to being engulfed by a cult.

In *Delusion* we see how the trap was set for one little girl and her family. Her memories and family stories reveal how powerful the need really is to belong. It is a revelation of how much they were willing to surrender in order to be a part of the group. It happened right here in the United States! These family members were industrious, intelligent, compassionate, God-fearing people. But the lack of discernment brought broken relationships, heartache, despair, and even death.

Patricia Hochstetler is finally telling her story. This book is a glimpse of how easy it is to be drawn into the dangers and despair of a cult. This book is the first of a three-part series: Deception is exposed in book two and deliverance is revealed in book three.

Paul S. Trittin
Publisher

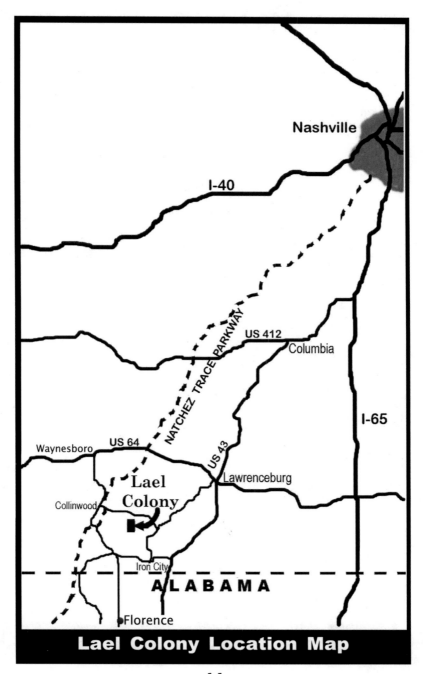

Lael Colony Location Map

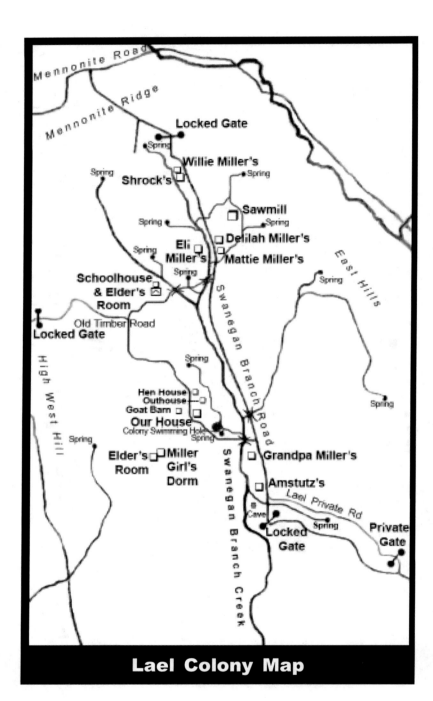

Lael Colony Map

Chapter 1

Stepping Away

"Goodbye, Grandma. Goodbye," I cried as I waved and stepped away.

The truck was loaded with all our belongings when my family and I crawled in, and we left. Dad drove all day and into the night long after dark. As I slept, I was awakened to the crash of our truck.

It was after midnight, and while we children had been sleeping Dad drove up an inclining, curvy, gravel road. When the truck could no longer pull the heavy load, he tried to back down those curves in the dark. Suddenly the back wheel on the passenger side ran off the road, and the truck rolled onto its side. Small trees prevented it from rolling onto its top and down the embankment.

Fred, my brother, had been asleep with his head on Mom's lap. He flew off her lap and cut his head on the popped-open glove box. My sister, Joan, and I were in the back of the tarp-covered truck along with Teddy, our dog. Dad had taken the back window out of the truck's cab and made a bed for us in the middle of the furniture. Our bed lay on top of two huge barrels of glass jars filled with canned food. God protected us, for miraculously we were unhurt.

Dad climbed out the driver's window. From inside the truck Mom handed us children to him, and then he helped Mom out. Without a house in sight they pulled blankets from the truck and bedded us and the dog on the ground in the black, early morning darkness. I couldn't see my hand in front of my face except when flashes of lightning streaked across the sky allowing us a glimpse of our damaged truck laying on its side. Thunder followed, signaling a threat to soak us. I felt Mom's touch as we huddled on the blankets and listened to her reassuring voice. The sound of Dad's footsteps crunching off into the distance weakened as he left to seek help. As lightning and thunder continued, it began to sprinkle.

It seemed a long time before Dad returned. I awakened when he and Mom spoke briefly.

"Mary, I walked at least two miles, and I didn't see a sign of people anywhere," Dad reported.

"My biggest concern is to get Fred to a hospital and get his head stitched up before going on to the colony. I know we can't see a doctor there," Mom replied. "I'm very thankful nobody else is hurt, our truck looks drivable, and it seems there are only a few pieces of furniture broken."

Dad bedded down with us for the rest of the night. The rainstorm eventually passed, and we waited for morning's light. Just before dawn with us children asleep on the ground, Mom and Dad were unloading their furniture when a car stopped.

"Ya need help?" the man asked.

"Yes! I need to get my boy to a doctor, and I'll need a wrecker to pull our truck up," Dad answered.

"I'll take ya to the hospital and to get a wrecker. First I need ta go home and let my wife know where I'm at. Jump in!" The stranger motioned for us to climb in.

We rode a few miles with Joan and me on Dad's knees and Fred in Mom's arms. At the man's home we were greeted warmly by his wife.

"Hon, meet the Long family. They wrecked down on the hill and need help, and I'm tak'n 'em to the hospital."

"I think the little girls and the dog should stay here with me while ya take their parents to get some help for that little boy and take care of business," the stranger's wife said. "Ya kin leave 'em here with me if that's aw right."

The man turned to Dad and asked, "Would that be aw right?"

Dad looked at Mom. When she nodded yes, he turned

to the man and said okay. It was a little scary, but Mom said we would be all right. So Joan and I stayed behind and enjoyed a good breakfast.

As Mom tried to comfort Fred, the stranger spoke to Dad. "We'll take your wife and boy to the hospital, and then we'll find a wrecker so you can head back to your truck. As soon as the doctor is finished, I'll bring them back here to the house."

Dad nodded in agreement, and Mom got into the truck. Dad handed Fred to her, climbed in, and they left for town.

While Mom waited at the hospital for the doctor to put some stitches in Fred's head, the stranger took Dad in search of a local garage. They found a man who had a wrecker, and he and Dad were soon on the way to our truck. The stranger returned to the hospital, picked up Mom and Fred, and returned to his home.

When they arrived from the hospital, these generous, helpful strangers took us back to the accident scene. Our truck was back up on the road, and people were helping Dad reload. Even with multiple dents and scratches our truck still ran okay. Resuming our journey, we found the general area where we were supposed to meet Christian Amstutz twenty-four hours later. Because we were so early, Dad tried to find the valley and colony people himself. Frustrated, he eventually parked near the woods, and we waited the rest of that day. We ate some of our canned food. When night finally came, sleepy children had to be cared for.

"Where're we gonna sleep, Mommy?" I asked.

"Where we gonna sleep?" Joan whimpered.

"Well, when the truck got loaded again, you lost your bed. We'll just have to make some other arrangements," Mom answered in a comforting tone.

"God's earth is good and solid," Dad noted.

"Clarence Long, I am *not* sleeping on the ground and neither are these children."

"We slept on the ground last night, Mary," Dad countered.

"That was then and this is now. My parents warned

me about the rattlesnakes in this area."

"I'll sleep on the ground," Dad mumbled. "I'm not scared of snakes."

Dad considered the discussion over, but Mom had a bit more to say. "I'll fix a place for the girls on the truck seat. Teddy can sleep with them to help keep them warm."

"Where you gonna sleep?" Dad challenged.

"You're gonna help me get on top of the tarp-covered furniture. Then you're going to pass Fred up to me. We'll be safe up there."

The decision was made, and there was nothing more to be said. Mom got on top of the truck, and Dad handed Fred to her. Dad found a spot on the ground, and everyone settled down for the night.

How did all of this get started? What had caused us to end up here?

I was born in Elkhart, Indiana, to Clarence K. and Mary (Miller) Long. My parents wanted the best for me and tried to protect me from the evil in the world around them. They wanted a better life for their children than the ones they had. That choice meant exile for me and my siblings in a colony far away from what my folks considered to be an ungodly society.

Mom, raised Amish, could not speak English when she started school. The second daughter of fifteen children born to Benjamin and Elizabeth (Amstutz) Miller, she was born in Bayminette, Alabama, in 1928. Her childhood was spent feeding animals and poultry on their farm. Everyone was expected to help support the family. Planting, cultivating, and harvesting crops by hand and with mules were part of her routine. She helped her father harvest the sap from pine trees which they distilled and sold as turpentine or used for salve.

At age fourteen, in 1942, her dad sent her outside their home to do housekeeping and farm chores for another family. The mother of that family had a broken leg. By then Mom's younger sisters were old enough to do the work at home. All the money she made went to her father to help feed their very poor family.

Contrary to Amish tradition Mom never had a *rumsprunga*, the running around time for Amish children after age sixteen. Her father did permit her to work in a factory, and from the money she earned he gave her one-dollar per week allowance for personal expenses. The rest was kept to help feed her brothers and sisters.

At eighteen, Mom, her oldest sister, Naomi, and her Aunt Delilah Miller ventured to Elkhart, Indiana. Their Aunt Amanda Miller, cousins, and other relatives lived among the Amish in Middlebury which wasn't far away, and Uncle Jacob Schrock lived in Fort Wayne.

Mom enjoyed working the day shift sewing at Smolers dress factory in Elkhart. During the evenings and on weekends she worked as a waitress in the Dixie restaurant at the Elkhart Hotel. Until she and my dad were married she continued sending most of her money home to help feed her siblings.

While attending classes at the Elkhart School of Business, my dad managed the night shift at the Dixie, and that's how he met Mom. He was first attracted to her because of her Amish background. He often reflected about the time he went to elementary school in the small town of Etna Green, Indiana. It was the Amish children there who treated him kindly while most of the other students made fun of him. Since then, he always liked the Amish.

Dad was the second child born to Frank and Bertha (Livengood) Long. Their first baby died at birth. After Dad they had three more children. The last two were twins. Grandfather Long was an extremely jealous man, an alcoholic, and abusive. As a child, my dad faced some horrible things, the most serious when he was only eight.

According to a newspaper article the police believed Grandfather Long was John Dillenger, a dangerous criminal who was often in the area. When they stopped him, he began shooting at them. They riddled his car with bullets, but amazingly he survived the gunfire. He was arrested, treated for his many gun shot wounds, and put in prison. He had a vengeful attitude and continually threatened those around him.

He remained in prison for years until they moved him to a veterans hospital where he eventually died. Though he never returned home, Grandma Long remained faithful to him. I never knew my Grandpa Long, but Mom claimed he always referred to me as his little Annie, after his sister, Annie.

After the shoot-out, Dad, his mom, and three younger siblings moved from Etna Green to Elkhart, Indiana, to be near his Grandpa and Grandma Livengood and other relatives. During those formative years many children in Etna Green and Elkhart were unmerciful in their scorn as they made fun of him because his dad was in prison. The Amish children were different. They helped him and were kind in spite of his circumstances.

Dad and his family faithfully attended a local Pentecostal church. When he was fourteen, he went to the altar, repented, and accepted Christ as his personal Savior.

Eventually he and his two brothers enlisted and served in the military until World War II ended. After boot camp in San Diego, California, he remained there to serve as a guard at the Naval Base before being stationed in Maui, Hawaii. Later he was transferred to the artillery where he maintained and repaired weapons.

When Pearl Harbor was bombed, Dad's Marine Corps unit was sent there on a rescue mission. He pulled many wounded and dying men out of the water. Whenever he talked about his time in the service, he always added, "I was never on the battlefield, and I never killed anybody!"

After receiving an honorable discharge from the military in 1945, he returned to Elkhart where he met Mom in 1946. This was about the time she received a letter from her parents that would drastically change their lives.

"The Amish church is using a *mieding* (shunning) on your grandfather, Moses Amstutz. The church put a *bann* on him. Then a great Jewish leader came to us and we followed him. His name is Mack Sharky. We believe he is a true man of God. He told us to shake hands with your grandfather so the church would excommunicate us. He claims that the Bible says to honor our parents, and it's not honoring them to shun them. So we invited them for dinner and shook hands with him and your grandmother, and our church has excommunicated us now. This leader has delivered us from the Amish church and is teaching us Bible truth. He quotes the Bible from cover to cover by memory. We believe he is the only true prophet of God. He says it is okay to marry outside the Amish people and not to shun those who do."

Grandma's letter set Mom free to marry outside the Amish church knowing that she would not be shunned or cut off from her family. Mack Sharky approved of her getting married. Dad told people they were going to be married, and he gave her an engagement ring. Mom declared she barely knew him, yet felt she couldn't disappoint him so she kept the ring. Now that Mom was engaged she took a bus to Aberdeen, Mississippi, to visit her parents, her nine brothers and sisters, and her other Amish relatives. A highlight of the trip was the opportunity to meet the Jewish leader her parents were following.

Mom stayed with her family and told them about her engagement. On Sunday morning she put tape around her engagement ring to hide it from the disapproving Amish at the Amish Church of God. This is the church Mom grew up in, was baptized in, and became a member of at age twelve. She felt happy to see everybody.

Abruptly Ananias Schrock, the Amish preacher, asked an unsettling question, "Have you used a *mieding* on your parents?"

When Mom answered "No," he said, "Because of that testimony you are excommunicated from the Amish Church of God."

Mom concluded that since she was no longer a member of the Amish church this must be preparation for joining the

Jewish leader's group along with her parents. They sincerely believed Mack was a true man of God. During this time Dad had been reading the book, *Five Acres and Independence,* which made him even more eager to be with the Amish on farmland. Mom's only reservation surfaced when she realized she would not be allowed to ever take her children to any doctor or dentist.

Two months after she returned to Indiana Mom and Dad were married in a small, quiet ceremony in a preacher's home. It was the fall of 1946 just three months after they had met at the Dixie restaurant.

Later Dad quit the Dixie restaurant and started a partnership with his brother, Carl, but because of Carl's alcoholism, that business didn't last long. Dad went to work at Miles Laboratories. They were so impressed by his ability and work ethic that they sent him to engineering school.

About a year after my mom last saw her family and on her nineteenth birthday, she gave birth to her first baby, Fred Benjamin Long, who bore the name of both grandfathers. It was July, 1947. When Fred was six weeks old, Mom took a bus from Indiana to Mississippi to again visit her family. She met her ten-month-old brother, Enos, who barely survived the birthing ordeal. Their mid-wife honored the church *bann* on them and would not help with the delivery. This forced my grandfather to turn Enos before birth. Their new leader named him Enos Micah insisting that he have a middle name. No other child in our family had a middle name.

Mom proudly presented Fred, the first grandchild in her family. He had screamed with colic the entire trip, and people on the bus complained. By the time she reached her family she was exhausted! Things didn't improve a great deal after that. Unfortunately she couldn't hear the new leader's teachings when attending a meeting because she had to take Fred out and walk down the dirt road far enough so his voice didn't disturb the service.

When she returned home to Elkhart, she and Dad purchased about two acres in a suburban area. Dad designed a house and garage to build for his growing family. He built the garage first, and they lived in it while he continued building the house as he could afford the materials.

The next year in June, 1948, I was born and named Patricia Ann Long. Aunt Naomi came and stayed at our home for a week to help Mom. Just a year later in June, 1949, my sister, Joan Ellen Long was born. By this time Mom's sister, Naomi, and her Aunt Delilah had returned to Mississippi to live with the colony and follow the Jewish leader.

My parents now had three children in less than three years. Knowing they would follow the Jewish leader and take their children into isolation, they did not expose us to much of the world. They eagerly waited for instructions as to when they would be allowed to enter the colony.

At ages one, two, and three, Mom and Dad took us to Hamilton, Mississippi, in their 1946 burgundy Studebaker Champion to visit the colony. Dad, my sister, and I met Mom's family and the colony leader for the first time. The next year we went to visit again. My aunts made dresses for Joan and me and a shirt for my brother. We attended their Sabbath meeting and heard the Jewish leader's teachings. We also explored their private school.

During the four years the colony lived on the Hamilton land, they had harvested much timber and cleared many fields for farming. Unfortunately The Elder became displeased because Amish relatives were occasionally visiting the colony's young children who were not previous members of the Amish church. To eliminate this intrusion he ordered the colony to sell the Hamilton land and move to a more isolated place farther away from their Amish relatives. This decision caused the leader to put my parents' move to the colony on hold until a new location was selected.

Dad was becoming anxious. "We've waited almost four years to join the colony, and I want to be settled before the children start school," I had heard him complain.

Mom nodded and expressed similar feelings.

"Mary, I'm eager to step away and disappear from here. I want to live where I can cut timber and work on the farm with the Amish people and get away from the pressures here.

I want to follow the prophet of God and learn God's ways."

"It won't be long now," Mom answered, "before we can learn God's truth."

Chapter 2

The Amish-Jewish Colony

His appearance should have been enough to raise suspicions. A black felt stovepipe hat in Aberdeen, Mississippi, any time of the year was a misfit, but in the spring of 1946?

The whole country was still in transition. His dust-covered hat, his dark plaid shirt, and his black pants were a sure sign he hitchhiked into town, but that wasn't too uncommon. Cars were not seen too frequently even though the war ended several months earlier.

"Where do the good people live in this town? I mean the Amish." He never used his name, but Mack Sharky had arrived.

The town's merchants compared notes. "Have you seen 'im?" They all knew the "him."

"Looks to me like he might be 'bout the late fifties like us," one merchant volunteered.

"Yep, he's pretty mature for a hitchhiker. Seems a bit too old to be a veteran though," another added.

"Wonder where he came from," the first man muttered, and the locals moved on to other topics.

Eventually Mack Sharky received his answer.

"Oh, the Amish live out thata way," a shopkeeper said as he pointed north.

According to The Elder he walked out of Aberdeen in that direction until he came to a fork in the road. *Which way? To the right or left?* he wondered.

"Jehovah Jireh were the words I prayed," he later related to those who would listen. "I reminded the Lord that

His Word says the steps of a good man are ordered by the Lord. At that exact moment God sent a strong whirlwind which blew me toward Egypt Road, and I walked on that road until I saw Amish children in a yard and stopped there."

It was warm that day, and the Amish children playing in the front yard belonged to Abraham and Lydia Schrock. When the stranger arrived, they quickly ran into the house and told their mother that a strange man was in the yard. From the safety of the house they watched as he walked right up to the door and knocked. Their mother was holding Josephine, her newborn daughter, when she opened the door.

"Greetings in the name of Christ Jesus, The Lord, whom *I* serve. I am a Nazarite and a servant of God. I want to come in and speak with you," the stranger boldly announced. Lydia, being a bit apprehensive about letting the man in, talked to him at the door.

After a brief exchange and noticing she was still uncertain, he commented, "That little baby in your arms is a precious bundle."

She weakened and invited him in.

Once inside he was even more bold. "With your consent I would like to remain here until I may speak to your husband." Having made that statement he took a seat in the front room.

According to Barbara, one of the daughters of Lydia Schrock, the stranger tried unsuccessfully to interact with the children, but they were shy and watched and listened from nearby as he chatted with their mother.

Sharky was calm, extremely aware, sure of himself, and yet unapproachable. He didn't really scare anyone, yet there was something very different about him, like a man from another world. His walk was deliberate and meaningful, a man with a purpose, almost like a dignitary or someone of authority. He was a person who claimed his space! He seemed like a man on a mission who felt he had found his calling.

In her own kind, caring way Lydia Schrock chatted

with the man and offered a glass of water. He was forward enough to inform her he had not eaten for some time and anything light would be okay — except he didn't eat pork. For everything she offered he had a reason why he couldn't eat it. The drop biscuits left from lunch had lard in them. Pork may have been cooked in the pans she used for making gravy, and he made some remarks about vegetables and oils. He finally decided scrambled eggs would be all right served with bread which had a kosher sign, a circled K, on the label. He wanted the bread plain, no butter or jelly, and toasted in the oven not in a skillet.

Was he dangerous? Was he truly a man of God as he claimed? These were valid questions to ponder under the circumstances. They were even more frightening when after eating he claimed to be tired and wanted to rest there. With some reservations Lydia permitted him to remain in the front room until her husband came home.

Abraham was in for a surprise.

"Greetings in the name of Christ Jesus, The Lord, whom *I* serve. I am Mack Sharky, an orthodox Jew from Pittsburgh, Pennsylvania. I left my Jewish family and ancestry, and I became a Nazarite and a prophet of God who sent me to your people, the Amish, and directed me to you." He scarcely paused before quoting many Bible verses, and then he asked Abraham with insistence, "May I stay tonight in your home?"

It was not long before there was no doubt that Sharky knew the Bible. During their lengthy conversation Abraham did the unusual thing and actually invited him to attend the Amish church on Sunday morning. A small house with eleven children made it easy to decline Sharky's request for housing for the night. But he mentioned that Benjamin Miller, his brother-in-law and my grandfather, might have room in his much larger new house. The two men went to my grandfather's home and the introductions were made.

Mack Sharky greeted my grandfather with the same words he did everyone else. "Greetings in the name of Christ Jesus, The Lord, whom *I* serve." Knowing that his brother-

25

in-law had invited the stranger to church in the morning, Grandfather allowed him to stay.

Sunday morning Mack Sharky ate breakfast with my grandfather's large family and rode to church on their wagon pulled by a team of horses. Mack commented, "I consider it a privilege to worship with the Amish."

In the service when Mack was introduced he stood to his feet and proclaimed, "I am a Nazarite, a servant of God who sent me here to you. In Numbers chapter six the Bible speaks of me. I eat no grapes and drink no wine. I never cut my hair or beard. I keep every day as a Sabbath. I have separated myself unto the Lord for the rest of my life. I have vowed a vow unto the Lord to be a Nazarite. I am holy, and . . ."

"Pardon me, my new brother," Ananias Schrock, the Amish preacher, interrupted. "The spirit has to be tried as 1 John 4:1 tells us. *Beloved, believe not every spirit, but try the spirits whether they are of God: because many false prophets are gone out into the world.* According to the Bible, which you profess following to the letter, 1 Corinthians 14:40 tells us to *let all things be done decently and in order.* So I shall now proceed with the morning message."

The stranger sat down in expressionless compliance, hands folded in his lap for the rest of the meeting. One person reported seeing a single teardrop rolling down the man's cheek and falling on his lap. It was not his self-ordained lot in life to be reproved or instructed. After the worship hour ended, polite, kind, and friendly, he shook hands with everyone he could. To each person he repeated, "Greetings in the name of Christ Jesus, The Lord, whom *I* serve."

Some reported he appeared to wait for the "holy kiss" reserved for members and seemed disappointed to only get a handshake. He quoted Bible verses and even chapters to the people, leaving a deep spiritual impression. He had a boldness and memory of the Bible the Amish lacked. After this experience many members opened their homes to him, and he was able to stay with different families.

One day Mack announced, "I will have meetings on Saturdays for those interested in hearing what I have to say." He began holding meetings in Amish homes every Saturday. He was careful to announce that all the Amish families were invited.

For awhile many attended his Saturday meetings and their own church on Sundays. He often declared. "I believe in the whole Bible, the Old and the New Testaments, not just the New Testament as some do! I teach the entire Bible. It's all God's Word. I especially teach to apply The Golden Rule, Matthew 7:12; to keep the Ten Commandments, Deuteronomy 5:6-21; and to observe The Dietary Laws in Leviticus 11:1-47."

As we were first getting to know him, Mack Sharky told everyone, "Only call me Mack. Never use Sharky. This will conceal my identity." Later he changed his request. "Call me Sharky only and not Mack." Then once again he changed his name to Ethan saying, "Nobody knows my real name." Over the period of twenty-three years he spent with the colony he changed his name several times: Mack Sharky, Mack, Sharky, Ethan, Uncle Ethan, The Elder, and his last name, Tav, which appears on his grave stone. He claimed Tav was the last letter in the Hebrew alphabet. To avoid confusion I have chosen to call him The Elder.

The Aberdeen, Mississippi, Amish originated from a group of Old Order Amish in Garnett, Kansas. They left in the early 1900's because of *rumsprunga* (running around) among the young people and issues they were unable to resolve. During this time of disunity some felt they should keep the Law of Moses, and this was written in *The Budget*, a public Amish newsletter. There was much dissatisfaction among them, and the group splintered into several clusters. My forefathers moved from Kansas to Arizona, and on to Oregon, Illinois, Indiana, Michigan, Ohio, Alabama, Mississippi, California, Florida, and to Gibson, Mississippi. They finally moved to Aberdeen, Mississippi, where The Elder appeared and caused another split.

Our group, Lael Colony, consisted of the adult children

who had been shifted around from state to state with their unsettled parents. They were considered by the Old Order Amish as *die hoch gonga leit* (the high gone people) meaning they strayed to modern things or went worldly.

With his Bible knowledge and strong Biblical pull The Elder soon had 75 percent of that Amish Church of God committed to following him, and they quit attending their church on Sundays. A comment by a previous member was on target when he said, "The church is ripe for a split because of dissatisfaction."

After careful analysis the Amish preacher made a decisive pronouncement, "All those who choose to follow Mack Sharky, the Jewish man, are excommunicated from The Amish Church of God, and we will immediately put a strong *bann* (ban) on them. All members of this church must use a *mieding,* (shunning) on them starting now. They are not to communicate, eat at the same table, or shake hands with the people they are avoiding with a *bann.*"

The Amish and *The Sharkys* both grew stronger in commitment to their own views. All the children still attended the same school.

The Elder, with his group now established and excommunicated from the Amish church, was not silent. "I fervently stress that you keep the first commandment with a promise: *honor thy father and mother* as it says in Ephesians 6:2 and in Deuteronomy 5:16, *that thy days may be prolonged, and that it may go well with thee, in the land which the Lord thy God giveth thee.* I admonish the Amish who wrongfully treat their parents by shunning them. According to the Bible this treatment is not right or honoring to parents."

Meanwhile The Elder began teaching his people about the Day of Atonement, and the Jewish laws, feasts, and fasts. He combined these with their Amish traditions and faith, some of which he altered. He confided, "I want you, my group, different from the worldly Jews and worldly Amish. You cannot be a born Jew as I am, but you can be converted Gentiles who can become Jews and God's chosen people." His followers strove earnestly to pursue their new leader's orders and to be God's people. They were given a choice to follow The Elder or reject him.

Abraham Schrock announced, "I chose to follow Sharky because I was quite dissatisfied with the Amish church before he came. The Amish made people do things I felt was unnecessary like changing the siding on their houses when it looked like four-inch siding and it was a grooved eight-inch board. This was considered deceitful. One had to look on the backside of the boards to tell the difference. When we bought a house and the roofing had fancy colors or design in it, we had to change the entire roof. I couldn't see doing that. Sharky had some good things, and he knew the Bible better than anybody I ever met. I thought I could live with his ways and beliefs, but I did have some questions. I didn't understand why he didn't believe in baptism as a symbol of following Christ. Yet he believed in physical circumcision as a sign of our covenant when I thought the Bible meant circumcision of the heart."

On the contrary, Annie Schrock Luker Lee, a former Amish schoolteacher said, "I chose not to follow Mack Sharky. He knew the Bible cover to cover very well, but I questioned some of the ways he said to apply it. Our barn was across the road from our house, and he reprimanded our family because we called the men folks to dinner or called our animals. He said there was no need to holler so loud. He even demanded we sell all our hogs. Yet in the New Testament it says in 1 Timothy 4:3-5 that a man can eat all flesh if it be received with thanksgiving. 1 Corinthians 8:8 backs it up. That includes *de sie flaish* (the pork flesh) which The Elder was totally against.

"He talked mostly about himself. He spent a lot of days in our home, and I asked him many questions. One thing in particular helped me make up my mind. I asked him, 'Suppose a small baby that couldn't walk was in that crib and this house caught fire and there was nobody around but you to save the baby. Would you save the innocent child by carrying it out of the house?'

"Sharky's answer was, 'I'm afraid not because of my

Nazarite position with God which causes me to keep every day as a Sabbath.' This question was one of the determining facts that kept me from following Sharky."

Mose and Millie Miller had a different story. "We chose to follow Sharky and tried to do what he said, but we were never approved by him to join the colony. We left the Amish to join Sharky's group, and for five years he wouldn't tell us if he would allow us in or not. Finally we had to make a decision for ourselves because he never would tell us. We moved back near Aberdeen, Mississippi, where our children started school. We were never accepted by the Sharky's or by the Amish after that. By double rejection we were forced to make a life for ourselves. Now we count our blessings that God allowed us to get out and stay out of both groups. We became free to choose for ourselves."

Tension between the Amish and the Sharkys grew quickly. As it did, The Elder gave this added advice, "I encourage all the families who will truly follow me to sell your homes and farms. We will buy a plot of land and start our own village away from Aberdeen and the influence of your Amish relatives."

Christian Amstutz believed in The Elder, but his wife, Lizzie, did not. He sold their house and followed the orders from his leader. Meanwhile his pregnant wife and his oldest child who had joined the Amish church stayed in Aberdeen with Lizzie's parents. Christian took their other eight children ages two to thirteen with him. He missed the birth of his next child who was called "The Baby" for a year until a name was chosen. Eventually Lizzie could not stand being away from her children and decided to follow her husband and The Elder.

During 1947 and 1948 all The Elder's followers sold their homes and farms in Aberdeen and together they purchased 1,500 acres in Hamilton, Mississippi, several miles on the other side of Aberdeen. The colony moved their belongings, including animals, onto the land which had several old, run-down houses and barns. Much of the land was raw and covered with paper-pulp pines. The men began harvesting the trees immediately. Sabbath meetings were held in homes. They set up their own private school, and Delilah Miller, Grandfather's sister who had taught at the Amish school, was appointed teacher.

The families worked together and soon had large gardens in the rich soil. They were able to can ample supplies of food and vegetables for the winter. Under The Elder's instructions they bought a bulldozer and pushed out the stumps, relieving their mules of the hard work and speeding up the job of creating new farmland. Soon enough land was cleared for adequate farming. Each family had a field of cotton to care for and helped each other as needed. The colony seemed to adjust well and believed this was God's will for their lives and for the group as a whole.

The Aberdeen Amish relatives came to Hamilton occasionally and tried to influence adults through the children who had never become members of their Amish Church of God and consequently had not been shunned. The Amish conversed with the children, asking them to relay messages to their families. One time they drove onto the land and Christian Amstutz caused quite a ruckus when he parked his truck crosswise in the road so they couldn't get out. One of the Amish declared, "You Sharkys use a much harder *mieding* (shunning) than we do."

After four years much of the timber on the Hamilton land was harvested. At the same time The Elder became displeased that the Amish continued to visit his colony, so he issued a new ultimatum. "Sell this Hamilton land and move to a more isolated place farther away from your Amish families. Abraham Schrock, go to town and get newspapers and land magazines and watch for several hundred acres of land within a five state area."

The Hamilton land sold quickly to a neighbor without advertising and for a very large profit. "Keep this sale secret from the Amish community," The Elder ordered. "Abraham, you and Christian Amstutz, go look at the land for sale in Arkansas, Alabama, and Tennessee where school laws are lax. Then report back to me."

In 1951, The Elder chose a 2,005 acre tract of land in Wayne County, Tennessee. He proclaimed, "God revealed that this is the property He wants for His people. The acreage is timber-covered and filled with many huge oak trees. It is very hilly and has about seven high ridges and valleys. We can live near the creek that runs through the middle. God has given us this land flowing with milk and honey. Be thankful! Buy this land near Iron City, Tennessee, as a colony and put Oak Valley Farms on the deed."

Later The Elder named the school Lael Parochial School and called the group Lael Colony. He ordered that the land deeds be changed to Lael Valley Farms. The Hebrew word, Lael, meaning devoted to God, is found in Numbers 3:24. The Elder said, "You can refer to Lael Valley as 'The Valley.' Then nobody can find our location. We will get a colony post office box in Florence, Alabama, under one person's name so we cannot be traced."

When the colony purchased the Tennessee land The Elder commanded, "Abraham, you, your son Moses, and Willie Miller are to go ahead to clear the new property and on the north end set up a sawmill for making lumber to build houses and barns." The three men went to the new location and pitched a tent on the north end. They chopped their way through the wilderness with machetes, axes, and saws, and set up the sawmill.

One old house sat on the south end of the land facing east. Swanegan Branch Road ran in front of the house and Swanegan Creek flowed behind it. The Christian Amstutz family soon moved into that house. Separate houses were built for other colony families. A schoolhouse was constructed, and The Elder gave the orders, "I've named the school Lael Parochial School. You are to build an adjoining room on behind it for my living quarters."

The Elder divulged the plan for our departure. "I will release one family at a time to move into The Valley. Pack your belongings during the day, and then load them on the truck after dark to prevent anyone from seeing what is happening. Leave before daylight so there is no chance of being seen by anybody." Each family left when given permission by The Elder until all the families had disappeared without telling anything to their Amish relatives or any other people in the neighboring community.

Suddenly my great grandparents, Daniel and Nancy Miller, discovered seven of their eleven children and many grandchildren were missing without a trace. Great Grandmother walked around for weeks with her *schnupduch* (handkerchief) in hand crying and grieving. She wailed, "Dan, Dan, *voa sinn unsa kinna un de grosskinna?* (Where are our children and the grandchildren?)"

"We must keep praying every day that God will return them to us safe," Great Grandfather choked out. "I'm afraid they went somewhere with that false prophet, Mack Sharky, that the Bible speaks of in 1 Timothy 4."

Falling into a deep depression, Great Grandmother was forced to give up finding her children and grandchildren. All were well hidden with their Jewish leader and his colony. Swanegan Branch Road was the only road on the land and ran north to south nearly through the center of the property. The Elder closed it. "Put up large gates with locks on both ends of the road that come onto the land. That will prevent any strangers or relatives from entering the colony. Make a secret and private dirt road with a locked gate on the east side for colony use only."

While all this was happening my family in Indiana eagerly waited for our acceptance under The Elders instructions. We were prepared to join the colony near Iron City, Tennessee.

Chapter 3

Entering Lael Colony

"I'm quitting my job now," Dad announced, "and I won't take that last test."

"It seems like a shame not to take the last test. Miles Laboratories is paying for it. Why don't you take the test and then quit work?" Mom asked.

"Nope! I'll never use that operating engineer degree, so I'm quitting," Dad muttered. "I'm anxious to go live with the colony where I'll be free. I'm never going to be back here anyway."

The Elder sent word for my family to come on a particular date. But he canceled it for unknown reasons and left us waiting to hear from him as to when we were allowed to come. Dad had quit his job and impatiently waited for the command to move. He did odd jobs for neighbors and others in the area for two months. I remember him building an outside fireplace for Mr. and Mrs. Hasbrooks who asked my family to join them for dinner once Dad completed the job. This was the only time I remember eating at anybody's house. I recall walking there wearing an aqua dress that Mom had crocheted for me. On the way Mom informed us children, "Be polite. Wash your hands before going to the table. Be quiet. Say please and thank you. Eat all the food I put on your plates, and say may I be excused before leaving the table." This was the first time I had heard these commands.

Mr. Hasbrooks greeted us warmly. "Your children look like stair steps." Pointing at me he added, "I'm calling that one little Mary because she looks just like you, Mary."

Why doesn't he think I look some like my dad too? I

wondered. *Do I really look just like my mom?*

Most of the time we children stayed home with Mom in our simple one bedroom, gray cement block garage house that Dad built. Our home faced north, and we entered our only door at the northeast corner. Inside there was a tiny hall with a curtain to the left leading to our living room in the front. It had one window on the front and one on the west. The kitchen was open to the living room and had an inside wall separating it from our bedroom. A wire strung over head with a draw curtain from the inside wall to the east wall gave privacy to our bedroom. Mom and Dad's bed sat in the middle. A homemade bunk bed in the corner served as the bed for Fred and me. Fred slept in the top bunk and I in the bottom until Mom give the baby crib to her parents for my uncle Benja. Then Joan slept with me in the bottom bunk. A coal and wood burning stove stood by the inside west wall.

Mom used a kerosene two-burner oven combination for cooking and baking and an icebox for cooling stuff. A hand pump in the east side yard provided water. An outhouse on the hill behind the house served as our toilet by day, and at night we used a white enameled pot stored under our bed. In our front yard stood a homemade single swing with plenty of natural sand and sand burs around it. We had no phone. This small home is where my parents lived at my birth.

"Clarence, Patricia is the quietest baby I've ever known," Mom declared one day. "I often must wake her for feeding."

"Is she okay?" Dad asked.

"She seems fine," Mom assured, "but she just seldom cries. She's satisfied and very easy to care for."

"And that's a problem?" Dad asked jokingly. Mom ignored his comment.

Once after my sister was born Mom tried explaining why she was so tired. "Clarence, I put the children in our big, black, baby buggy and pushed them to a place I wanted to go in town. It's about five miles one way to Elkhart. I sat Fred and Patricia in the front side by side and lay Joan in the back. I took lunch along. I got really tired walking home pushing the buggy. With you working the second shift and sleeping late in the morning, I thought taking the children for a long ride after they ate breakfast would keep the house quiet so you could sleep better," she said.

Dad smiled his gratitude.

"Clarence, the time has gone so fast. I had three babies in diapers at once. Now Patricia is the first one trained. At eighteen months she's potty trained and doesn't have accidents. That surprises me. When I tried to potty train Fred, she understood and kind of trained herself," Mom said. "Patricia learns fast and talked young. Fred learned a lot of words from her. Of course, there's only eleven months between them. Joan's only a year younger than Patricia and is also learning a lot of words from her. Our children are growing fast."

As we grew older, some mornings we picked berries along a wooded area several streets behind our place until Dad woke up. Dad worked hard so he would be able to build a larger house for us beside our garage house.

Our tiny house and my family including Pal, our old black and white dog, and Cindy, our black cat, were about all I knew. I really liked our animals. They were almost like family members. When Cindy had three kittens, I quietly sat by her nest and watched them for hours.

Pal had been in our family as long as I can remember. He was everybody's friend. His floppy black ears, big brown eyes with a streak of white between them, and wagging black tail always said acceptance and love. His white paws were quick to run after any rag I threw. He could play but not me.

Pal was always there by our side. His black back became itchy with mange spots, which were curable, but my parents were practicing the "no doctor rules" and that also meant for Pal. Dad knew we couldn't take Pal with us into the colony with that disease. He had to do something before The Elder sent word for us to come live with the colony.

One morning Dad got up and solemnly whispered, "Mary, keep the children inside the house here with you for a while."

Dad disappeared.

Mom stayed busy with household duties, and Fred snuck outside.

Boom!

"Daddy, you killed my Pal," Fred screamed as tears began streaming down his face.

Dad came in and explained, "When I turned around with the rifle in my hand, I saw Freddie standing there. I felt so bad, but it was too late."

"Tricia, Daddy killed Pal," Fred cried out, and we cried together.

Our best friend, our Pal, our lifetime partner was dead.

Dad buried Pal way out in the back of our land. Mom tried to explain why this had to happen to our dog, yet it made no sense to us. For a long time we missed Pal by our side.

"I know I can't buy another dog once we move in with the colony," Dad told Mom. "I'll wait a few weeks and watch the ads in the paper and get another dog before we leave," Dad promised.

Dad bought us a blondish brown registered, tiny, toy Pomeranian we named Teddy.

"Look! I can carry Teddy," Fred shouted joyfully.

"I like Teddy's pointy little ears and his long hair that I can brush," I added.

Soon Teddy became like a family member, and he slept in our beds. Mom and Dad promised Teddy could go along with us when we moved. Grandma Long promised that Cindy and her kittens could stay in her garage when we left.

Sometimes Mom babysat for our cousin, Connie Scofield. Connie was seven months older than I. At age three I vividly remember having toothaches. One time Mom let me go along when she took Connie to a dentist appointment for Aunt Marie, Dad's sister. While in the waiting room, I heard Connie screaming. That scared me.

Mom sheepishly asked the dentist if he would look at my teeth knowing it wouldn't be long till we would be in the colony where dentists were not allowed. The dentist placed me in his big chair, and without a word I covered my mouth with my hands. His assistant then held my hands down scaring me more. Silently I pinched my mouth shut.

The dentist nodded to his assistant, "I'll fix her." He threw a full glass of water in my face. Water went up my nose and into my windpipe as I gasped. I coughed and cried. The dentist without ever seeing my teeth took me out of his chair and sent me to Mom in the waiting room.

I liked sweets and my toothaches continued. Dad liked candy and would buy it and say to me, "You can't have any candy because you have toothaches." That crushed me as I watched all the others eat candy.

One morning Dad went to the store, and I went to the swing in our front yard and sat there with a kitten in my arms. I waited and waited hoping today would be different and Dad would let me have candy. When he returned, he handed me a banana and tried to console me with, "You can have a banana instead of candy."

I felt so hungry I wanted to eat the whole thing. As I rolled the peels down on the banana, I wondered, *Why don't people eat the peeling?* I tried it. At first it tasted good as I ate the inside of the peeling. As I ate all the peel, I soon felt like vomiting. I quickly decided it is necessary to eat only the banana's fruit.

There weren't many neighbors. Bobby, who lived across the street from us, often rode his tricycle in their drive and that looked like fun. I was only allowed to watch him through our front window or from our yard. Reggie, a gadfly, lived east of us at the next cross street. He ran the neighborhood dirty and hungry almost everyday. Sometimes when he stopped, Mom would give him a sandwich and send him home. We weren't allowed to talk with or be around those boys.

As we prepared to leave for the colony, Mom took us children with her to say goodbye to Jerri Osborne, the neighbor who lived two houses east of us. Joan and I each received a tiny ceramic doll as gifts. I liked my baby doll that fit into the palm of my hand. I clutched her tightly and didn't let go. I sat quietly and admired my doll as Mom and Jerri chatted at the back door. Suddenly Joan snatched my doll from my hands saying, "My doll, mine."

Then Joan dropped my doll on the cement step and shattered it. I felt shaken, helpless, and disappointed. Jerri and Mom both saw this happen. Mom told Joan to find her doll and give it to me since she had broken mine. Joan found her doll in the grass, picked it up, and instead of giving it to me she threw it on the step shattering it also. Mom quickly told Jerri farewell. As we walked away, Mom declared, "You girls can't have dolls or take any when we move, so that solves the doll problem! I don't want to hear anymore about it. There are no dolls now."

My dream of having a baby doll was shattered just like my feelings. The kittens served as my babies. I spent hours each day swinging all the kittens on our homemade swing. I would pull twigs or weeds around behind me, and they chased them until I collapsed with a sand burr in my foot. Then the purring kittens circled me waiting until I had all the burrs picked out. The kittens played but not me; I worked as I entertained and babysat them. The swing became my escape. Of course if Joan came around I was usually forced to give it up.

"Clarence, Patricia is the one that likes the swing most," Mom said. "Of course she'll have to give it up when we move because it's too much like playing. Maybe we should take it down now."

"Okay," Dad agreed. "She has to learn to be without it."

A few weeks later Mom said, "Patricia, this is June 10. You were born four years ago today. Remember if somebody asks how old you are, you're now four years old."

"Okay, I'm four years old," I said holding up four fingers.

There was no celebrating, and I didn't miss it because I didn't know what that was. The main happening I remember on that birthday (the first one I remembered) was Mom holding our big, old, black, baby buggy as I climbed in, and then she let go and I rolled down the slope which seemed like a big hill at that time. We did this over and over. At first I wondered if I would roll beyond our west yard and out into the street. Mom assured me that the buggy would stop first, and it always did.

One day I heard Dad talking to Grandma. "Mom, you can tell the rest of our family that I'm moving to another state. I don't want my children raised in the tough atmosphere I grew up in."

Dad liked farming and the idea of living a simple life on the farm with Amish people seemed ideal to him. He waited eagerly each day for the orders from The Elder to join Lael Colony in the Tennessee Valley.

It was shortly after my fourth birthday that a letter came with The Elder's final approval telling my parents when and how to leave Indiana. He included a map and directions to go near the valley to an appointed spot where we would meet Christian Amstutz outside and away from the valley gates.

The cement block basement of our new house was completed, and Dad was ready to build the main level when my folks sold it so we could go to the colony. I remember seeing the man and woman that bought our place.

"Mary, come look! I traded our car for a 1946 black Chevy three-quarter ton truck. I've decided I can certainly find that Tennessee valley. We'll leave two days early so I have plenty of time.

The day before leaving, we loaded our belongings on the truck and covered it with a tarp. We took Teddy and spent the night at Grandma Long's house.

"Good bye, Cindy. Good bye, my babies," I said to each kitten in Grandma's garage. Some people came to see us and wish us well. Grandma seemed to know how to anticipate trouble, so she issued a warning.

"You children must stay out of the curtains."

As if on signal, Joan and another child rolled up in the curtains and spat through them. I wondered why they did that after being told not to. About that time Mom entered the room and saw what was happening.

"Fred, Patricia, and Joan sit down here until I say you can get up," Mom commanded. We all had to sit until the visiting people left even when only one of us had disobeyed.

"Clarence, can I please give the children some gifts I have for them?" Grandma pleaded. "Please! The gifts won't be wrapped."

"Okay," Dad muttered, "as long as there's no sign of Christmas."

Grandma gave Joan a boy doll, me a girl doll, and Fred a truck. Now I had a real doll, a perfect fit for my arms. The doll fit better than the kittens because they had grown so much. It appeared like Mom and Dad would let us take these gifts with us.

"Mary, my mom got by with that one. The children don't know that she bought the gifts six months earlier for Christmas. I wouldn't let her give them the gifts because we're living what The Elder teaches — not to celebrate any holidays or birthdays," Dad said.

"Girls, your dolls must stay in the boxes because it's against the rules to play with toys," Dad announced.

Mom and Dad let the dolls go with us to Tennessee, but I felt sad that Cindy and her kittens — which were my live babies — had to stay behind in Grandma Long's garage.

Before we left Elkhart the next morning, Grandma Long took a picture of us standing beside our loaded and tarp-covered truck. She assumed she would hear from us once we found a place to live in another state. She had no clue we would disappear, and neither did I.

My parents were following The Elder's instructions to deliberately mislead Grandma Long. Dad drove south over the northeast Arkansas state line, copied a letter written by The Elder, and mailed it telling Grandma where we were and the direction we were headed. The letter was to cause her to think we were headed southwest into Arkansas and that it was undecided where we would end up. That way she would have no idea what direction we actually went to join this most secret, well-hidden congregation.

Once the letter was mailed, Dad turned around as

instructed and went northeast toward Iron City, Tennessee. The sunset and that dark night settled on us.

A day and a half after our accident on the curvy road we met Christian at the appointed time and place. It seemed we followed him for miles over extremely hilly, rough, gravel roads and then dirt roads. Finally in a wooded valley we found the hidden colony and our Miller relatives.

"*Sis goot fa dich saina*" (It's good to see you), Grandpa said.

Now we were with God's chosen people and on the God-given land "that was to flow with milk and honey."

We stayed in Grandma and Grandpa Miller's full house the first few days. Then for sleeping, my parents set up a tent for us over toward Swanegan creek near Grandpa's potato house. The potato house was cool and had six-inch thick, sawdust-filled walls. Built to store vegetables and other foods it now served as our kitchen. This was our home while colony members and Dad cut timber, made lumber, and built our new house. The area was serene and quiet with clean air, fresh natural springs, rushing creeks, and singing birds. An indescribable peace filled the valley. A pure and perfect atmosphere it seemed. As a child of four, I felt I was in paradise.

Patricia Hochstetler

Chapter 4

Utopia

That summer of 1952 my family moved to Tennessee, and we were living in Lael Colony. The Colony's 2,005 acres were located just a hop south off Natchez Trace Parkway. Swanegan Branch Road ran through the middle of the acreage extending south off Railroad Bed Road on the north, Collinwood side, and continuing to Blackport Road on the south, Iron City, side. The village lay in the middle of a timberland jungle and in a deep, wide, and moist valley walled by a giant west hill and a very high east hill.

Welcomed by The Elder, his colony, and many of Mom's Amish family, we were happy to finally find them. What joy it seemed to enter Lael Valley and to have the privilege of becoming a part of Lael Colony — God's people — on God's land flowing with milk and honey. Still this four-year-old child did wonder why *we had to forget Elkhart, Indiana, everyone there, and everything that we knew before.* The fact there was one family still waiting outside the valley gates to be accepted did not concern me.

Being only a child and listening to the adults surrounding me, I felt I was one step from living in heaven, and the atmosphere seemed to prove it. The people referred to the land as the Garden of Eden, their utopia, and claimed they were living in bliss.

I overheard Grandpa say to Mom, *"Des himelich blatz nei de vellie iss von de Hawa.* (This heavenly place in the valley is from the Lord.) *Meah dank de Hawa.* (We thank the Lord.)"

I reached down and took a handful of the earth. The fabric of the soil was rough, rocky, and glazed with rich, moist compost. It was clothed with timber, threaded with sparkling, fresh creeks, and knotted with springs. I saw more land, woods, and water than I ever imagine existed. It seemed we were on a new earth or on the other side of the one we were on in Indiana.

Aunt Polly, who was just six years older than I, was expressionless when she remarked of the extreme stillness and butterfly quietness on our first ninety-five degree day. We walked through the woods and off in the distance we heard many singing birds and rushing creeks as we neared the village area. The earth there flourished with the beauty of nature. The air smelled as fresh and clean as a freshly-cut, ripe watermelon, and the transparent cold natural spring water tasted pure, smooth, and sweet.

"*Ya, vassa, vassa,* (Yes, water, water,)" Polly blurted pleasantly. "Yes, let's wet rags and hang them around our necks to cool off."

This helped a great deal as we wandered the land of paradise.

In this deep forest the sun seemed to crawl up over the treetops when it rose into view, and it sank behind the trees in the afternoon long before it set. We never saw a horizon sunrise or sunset in this valley.

Straight up through the web of trees the sky was a perfect picture of God's handiwork — clear blue sky sometimes etched with rolling cloud masses by day or the splendor of stars spangling overhead by night. We only saw the middle of rainbows; the ends hid in spaces beyond our wilderness.

Peace in the valley now flowed like the springs, streams, and creeks. Our many relatives surrounded us with care. We were all like a huge family working together in our gardens, cutting the timber, or at the sawmill. It felt good.

Saturday meetings held in family homes revealed to us The Elder prophet's rules and what he emphasized. The Elder with a twitch in his eyes rumbled, "I encourage you to learn God's laws better through my teachings. God has ordered some of your names to be changed to Bible names, and I will tell you whose names to change. Be of good courage now and fear God. Don't talk anymore than necessary. Then you will have no fear of saying anything wrong, and remember 'silence is golden'."

The Elder called my parents aside and said, "Clarence, God has ordered that your daughter's worldly birth name, Patricia, be changed to Lois, a good Bible name. Call her Lois! She is to try her best to have the faith of Lois in 2 Timothy 1:5."

Mom explained to me, "It's a privilege to have the servant of God choose to change your name to a Bible name, and your new name will be Lois. You need to try to be as good as Lois in the Bible and have her kind of faith. I'll read the Bible verses about Lois to you. You must remind people to call you Lois from now on." I had a strong desire to have faith like Lois in the Bible and to be the best person I could. I adjusted quickly to my special name.

One or two people's names were changed in most families, but I was the only one in mine. My Uncle Ed, only three months older than I was, had his name changed too. The Elder had changed it to Besodeiah meaning *in the secret of Jehovah*. It's used in Nehemiah 3:6.

That fall we were glad our house was completed, and colony members helped us move in before winter. The siding was black tar paper held up on boards by big round washers with a nail in each center. They tarred and then fastened tarpaper down on boards for our roof.

We moved into our new home—three bedrooms, living room, kitchen, and pantry. Our home was made from fresh green oak lumber harvested from the land of paradise, and all the walls remained bare studs inside except for the pantry which had thick, sawdust-filled walls. We had wood stoves in the living room and kitchen. This new home seemed huge compared to our garage-home in Indiana where my family all shared a bedroom. Now my sister and I shared a bedroom, Fred had his own and shared it with Teddy, and Mom and Dad had their own. Our beautiful new house had a south window in the living room near the front door. The back door went from the kitchen to a small back porch toward the creek.

We had plenty of yard to run in, woods to investigate, and trees to climb. One day while helping Mom in our garden, Fred said, "Here's a sprouted acorn. I'll plant it, and watch it grow. Someday I'll have my own big oak tree!"

During the summer many evenings after supper, Mom said, "Children come! We're going for a walk." She took along a bar of soap, a wash cloth, and a towel. We went to the colony's swimming hole for a good refreshing bath. The Swanegan creek swimming hole was halfway between our home and Grandpa's. Some of the older children dug it out on the eastside and left the other side shallow for us younger children. On the northwest side of the swimming hole stood an old, crooked, ragged-looking tree with roots like icicles reaching for the water. Under this tree is where snakes often lingered.

This creek ran beside our house and many times while swimming in the twelve to eighteen inch deep water, a snake would come swimming down the creek. We scrambled for the creek bank shouting, "Snake! Snake!" We constantly watched for water moccasins and rattlesnakes which were thick, especially in the fall. After swimming we always had to check our feet for bloodsuckers before entering the house. Sometimes the suckers were hard to remove, but they never stopped us from swimming.

One morning as we ate pancakes we spotted a black snake lying above the pantry door in the kitchen. "Children, sit still where you are!" Mom ordered.

We froze in our places at the table while Mom grabbed a broom, drew it back, and waited until the snake put its head on a flat spot. She whacked it as hard as she could causing the snake to tumble to the floor. Then she beat it to death. We developed a real fear and respect for all snakes even the rat snakes in the barn which only wanted to keep the rat population down and would not harm us.

Mom seemed like a snake expert because she knew the poisonous ones from the non-poisonous.

48

"I'll tell you children a snake story," Mom said. "When I was a young Amish girl I had the job of digging potatoes in a big field. My father always gathered rat snakes he found and put them in our barn to catch rats and mice, and he wanted his children to do the same. While digging potatoes I found a rat snake, chased it down, and held its head and tail under my shoes. I had no gunnysack or anything with me to put the snake in to take it home. So I unlaced my tennis shoe, took out the shoelace, and tied it around the snake's neck. I tied the snake up until I went home. Then I put the snake in our corncrib to catch rats and mice. When Grandpa found out what I did, he was very happy."

"Mommy, you're brave. I don't like snakes. They scare me, but I like you telling us stories. Will you tell another one?" I pleaded.

"Maybe tomorrow," Mom answered.

Entertainment for us was watching and helping Mom make biscuits. We took turns cleaning the big round silver-mixing bowl. What we didn't eat on the way to the creek, we rinsed in the creek to feed the minnows, and we watched them scramble for every bite. We spent hours trying to catch them for a closer look, and I investigated everything in and around the creek.

We also spent much time teasing a weed we called the shy weed. Some called it the mad weed, and others called it the sensitive weed. When we touched the weed, it folded up all its leaves like a prayer plant at night. It also folded up tight at night. By day it was open and awake until disturbed. It had soft, round, large marble-size flowers of lavender with light colored tips on the end of its spires resembling a porcupine.

The yellow love vine, which grew in large patches all over the valley, was another fascination. The vine wrapped itself around its neighbors in layers resembling a twine rope, and gripping so tightly it strangled the life out of all other vegetation around it, even colorful flowers such as dainty morning glories, tough cockleburs, and even small trees. It choked the life out of everything it touched.

There was also the passion plant which we called Maypops. Its delicate, colorful flowers yielded round, green, egg-size balls which turned yellow as they ripened to a sweet, tasty delight. It made a good snack anytime and anywhere.

Goats and cows were milked, eggs gathered, and we were always happy when Aunt Kay came to our home and said, "Here is extra cream from our fresh cows' milk for you to make butter or cottage cheese."

We liked the butter better made from cream off cow's milk than the cream from goat's milk. Aunt Kay usually stayed and joined in our evening chore and entertainment of passing the butter jar. We took turns shaking cream in a quart jar until it turned to butter for our pancakes or biscuits the next morning. One evening as we passed the jar, Aunt Kay informed us of what happened to her sister.

"Five days ago Erma was in a hurry when gathering eggs. She put her hand in a nest on top of a big coiled up rattlesnake, felt it, and quickly jerked back without getting bit. Erma feels extremely thankful she wasn't bit. The next night my father saw the same snake going down a hole, and he chopped it in half. Since then, we have seen the front half crawling around. We try to kill it, but it keeps getting away."

"Aunt Kay, I really enjoyed when you came to help Mom last week. Will you come again so I can take you down to the creek bank and show you our pet crabs? They live at the bottom of the creek? The water is clear and you can watch them walk on the bottom and use their big pinchers and long feelers."

"Sure I will." Later when Aunt Kay returned, she said they had finally killed the head half of the rattlesnake in their hen house.

I enjoyed spending the night at my grandparents. I liked to hear Grandma tell about the night that while Grandpa was still asleep he hitched up Pete and Henry, his mules. He woke up as he went to the field to plow. I always hoped to see him sleepwalk as he often did, but I never did. I slept with Aunt Kay in the upstairs bedroom she shared with her six sisters. Once in the middle of the night, I remember waking to the screaming of a chicken. My aunts hurried to the hen house. A possum was eating a hen alive starting on her bottom. The poor hen ended up on the dinner table by noon.

In the morning I was excited to go help milk their cows, *Bausy* (Bossy) and Beauty, and to feed the chickens and goats. I wanted to stay all day, but I always had to go home in the afternoon.

Sometimes we would walk to Aunt Lizzie's. She gave us a delightful treat, homemade wild grape jelly on leftover biscuits. Our Amstutz cousins showed us a small cave south of their house and on the east side of Swanegan Creek. I thought this cave was cool and nice and could easily be a summerhouse as someone suggested.

One day Grandma Miller in her blue apron wiped sweat from her brow as she slowly came walking barefoot down our dirt road leading Marlow, their billy goat. I ran down the road to meet her friendly face. "Grandma, Grandma, Marlow is peeing on your dress." I said.

"Unfashtanlich (unbelievable) Marlow." She backed up quickly and blurted, *"Net so do.* (Don't do that.)"

Grandma stopped for a minute to catch her breath and to answer my many questions as to why she was bringing Marlow to our house. She claimed he wanted to visit our goats while she visited Mom. She put Marlow in the barnyard, and we went to the house. Weeks later she came back to get Marlow. She never wore a coat or shoes that I can remember, yet she was always hot even if it was cool.

One time Grandma brought Uncle Benja, her youngest son and the youngest colony member. Grandma sat on a log visiting with Mom. We took turns straddling the log close beside her and putting our hands under her big fat armpits to warm them. She never seemed to mind and went on talking. She was the best, tenderhearted, kind, and warm, big round grandma I ever knew. I grew very fond of her and learned to understand all her Dutch words even though Mom thought there were words I didn't know. I especially listened when I heard Mom say, *"Sie kon sell net fashta.* (She cannot understand that.)"

By listening I often learned many things, and I never said a word about knowing what they were saying. I knew they would stop talking about some things around me if they knew. *Did Mom forget she had taught me Dutch words in Indiana even if we couldn't say them around Dad?* I wondered.

"Lois, you're four now. Would you like to learn to sew?" Mom asked one day.

"Sure."

"I will teach you to sew with a needle and thread first and then on the machine someday."

I nodded excitedly.

"You need something small to start with. Would you like to make clothes for Sarah, the doll Grandma Long gave you?"

"Am I allowed to?"

"Yes, if you don't play with her. You know playing is against the rules. But you will be working. You will be learning to sew and making clothes for Sarah like I make clothes for you. You can try her clothes on only once to see if they fit then you must put her and her clothes away."

I agreed, and I watched Mom take Sarah from her box on the high shelf in her bedroom closet. She looked at Sarah and quickly cut out a dress for her then put her away again.

"Mom, how can you cut out her dress without a pattern?"

"I look at her and guess."

"Will it fit her?"

"Once you sew the dress you can try it on her and see. I will thread your needle with a short thread so it won't tangle as easily. I'll knot the end so it won't pull through the fabric. You watch me so you can do it later." Mom added.

She was having some problems threading the needle and explained, "See how hard it is to get the thread through the eye of this needle? The Bible says that's how hard it is for a rich man to enter the gates of heaven. That's why The Elder tells us to be poor and satisfied not wanting anymore than we need.

"Now watch close. This is how you sew. Go down

through the fabric and come back up; then pull the needle and thread through like this. You only take one stitch at a time. I will pin the two pieces of fabric together, and you be careful not to stick yourself with the pins or needle."

"This is easy," I declared as I started stitching. I kept stitching until I was worn out. Mom told me to take a break. When I came back, it seemed even easier. I did not want to quit sewing. "Now I can sew like you, Mommy."

When the dress was sewn, Mom showed me how to sew buttons on. That was harder, but I mastered it.

"I will sew the button holes until you learn how to sew well," Mom insisted.

Sarah's dress fit. With Mom's help, I made her many clothes and stored them in a shoebox beside her box in Mom and Dad's closet. As we worked, Mom also taught me Psalm 23. This was the first chapter in the Bible I learned.

Time approached for Lael Parochial School to begin. The Elder, Delilah Miller, the teacher, and my parents decided I should start school at age four and go into first grade with my brother. Fred and I had a long walk to school. Mom walked with us to the first bend in the logging road and watched us walk to the next turn.

Aunt Dee, our teacher, or an older student watched us the last stretch until we arrived at school. I enjoyed school very much that year and remember learning to spell cat, dog, and even some five-letter words. I learned to read from the Dick and Jane readers. I would read to Mom in the evenings after supper until I was so tired I could not keep my eyes open.

"There will be tomorrow, and you can read more when you are not so tired. Now you must quit reading and go to bed." Mom whispered.

In my long nightgown, I would run from our living room with its oil lamp to my ink dark bedroom as fast as I could. I jumped in bed because I was afraid a snake would come up through the half-inch wide cracks between the floorboards. The house was built with green lumber and it dried leaving big cracks. I rolled up tight in my blanket and drifted off to sleep listening to the beautiful sounding whippoorwills. They also served as morning alarms, waking us before daybreak.

Each new day Mom did all she knew to make a good life for us children. She involved us in whatever work she did and tried to make it fun.

Chapter 5

The Elder and His Rules

Who was The Elder?

That is still a mystery! He freely admitted changing his name claiming, "Nobody really knows who I am!" Six times he ordered the colony members to address him by a different name. Why didn't that fact alone alert colony members? No one knows, but it does indicate the power The Elder was able to exercise over his followers. For what were the colony members seeking that caused them to be so easily brainwashed into submission?

The truth-seeking Amish who first encountered The Elder were deluded by this Bible-quoting stranger. Preying on their respect for the Scriptures, he used his pseudo-knowledge of Biblical truths for his own personal glory. Families who valued a good name above riches were duped into following a man whose name was unknown and his word unproven.

I had The Elder's name, Mack Sharky, researched and learned nothing. Search efforts in sections of the country where he claimed to have lived were unrewarding. The producers of *Unsolved Mysteries*, a one-time popular television program, expressed some interest, but there was no follow-up.

The Elder declared, "God leads me to do whatever I do. All the letters of my real name are here and there on that box," he said one time while staring at a cracker box. The Elder didn't tell what those letters were, and the people dared not ask because he didn't want to be questioned by anybody about anything.

He usually avoided things that led to personal questions, yet he liked to talk about himself and his achievements. Bits of information slipped through his lips during the twenty-three years he held rule over Lael Colony members, and the people gradually gained a smattering of information without his deliberate assistance.

There was something about Mack Sharky (or whoever he really was) that demanded attention. According to the merchants in Aberdeen, Mississippi, he appeared to be in his late fifties when he hitchhiked into their quiet little town in 1946. He arrived wearing a *zierote* (an ornamental), dark-striped, plaid shirt, black pants, brown work shoes, and a black felt stovepipe hat. His hands looked soft, unlike a working man's hands. He stood about six feet tall, thin framed, and weighed about 160 pounds.

He had salt and pepper grayish hair, and he neatly tucked his beard and his hair inside his shirt collar. His ears stayed hidden under big, puffy, course, lengthy hair. His long narrow nose had a distinct hump in it. His face had very few wrinkles on fair skin. His blue eyes showed friendliness accompanied by a blank expression. Words squeezed out from between his thin lips which gapped enough to show his missing and decaying teeth. The corners of his mouth neither turned up nor down with expression. His soft-spoken words were well put together in English.

With his head up The Elder walked erect and alert in the direction the town people had given him. He projected a sense of humility as he held his arms behind his back and gripped one hand with the other.

From the very beginning his power was unmistakable. The Elder schmoosed his way into the Amish homes and stayed. Claiming to be thirsty, The Elder found drink; hungry he found food; tired he was given a place to rest.

"God blesses people like you who provide for His servant," he often said.

His request for clean clothes was met, and somebody volunteered to wash his dirty and only suit of clothing. He was given a gray shirt, and he never wore his plaid shirt again. From that day on The Elder always wore black corduroy pants and jacket, a pilgrim-gray twill shirt, black socks, shoes, and felt hat. The Amish ordered a pair of black leather shoes he wanted. He requested his jacket be trimmed in dark navy blue ribbon to remind him to keep God's commandments. When offered a straw hat for daily use, The Elder said, "That's a work hat. I only wear a black felt, dress hat."

The Elder was not a man of tears. The only tear ever observed trickled down his cheek the first time he attended the Amish church and was asked to sit quietly and orderly. When it served his purpose, he acted like a quiet, humble, and docile man, but humility was really not one of his strong points.

Seeming to have a photographic memory, The Elder wooed the Amish with his superior Bible knowledge and memorization. His ability to read the Bible seemed superb. He stayed in the homes of many different Amish families and settled down among them but stayed hidden. His straight vertical and neat handwriting looked outstanding. But it remains a mystery why he refused to ever sign his name. He never had any identification and refused to carry anything in his pockets with the exception of a cloth handkerchief. He also refused to touch money or ever have it in his possession or on his body at anytime. He refused to drive any vehicles or do any kind of work.

It is difficult to understand how hard-working, conscientious people could be hood-winked into following a man whose work ethic seemed so different from their own.

He answered the *why* questions by saying, "I was called in 1937 to serve God. I am a Nazarite, a servant of God, and an apostle of God. God speaks to me. I have taken the vow of a Nazarite as in Numbers 6 for the rest of my life. I cannot cut my hair or beard. I eat no grapes, drink no wine, or partake of anything from grapes. I am a holy man that keeps every day as a Sabbath. Therefore I cannot ever work or carry anything in or out of any house or building."

More things leaked from The Elder's lips as time passed.

"My parents were Orthodox Jews and not originally from the United States of America," The Elder shared. "They spoke Yiddish, and they had some connections with the Ukraine. I never got along with my father, and I was fonder of my mother than my father. I remember nursing from my mother's breasts."

The Elder never revealed his age, his parent's names, or what happened to his father.

"My parents had nine children, and I was the middle child. The older children were born outside the United States, and I was the first one born here in the United States. I never got along with or liked my older brothers," the Elder declared.

The Elder never said where or when he was born or if he had ever obtained a birth certificate. He claimed to have a younger sister named Ellen who at one time lived in Akron, Ohio. He also spoke of his brother, Bill Sharky.

After the colony settled in Tennessee The Elder wrote to his brother, Bill, in Pennsylvania and had him send a bunch of King James Version Bibles to the colony's post office box in Florence, Alabama. Some colony members recall addressing that letter, and they received the Bibles. Bill and Ellen are the only two siblings that he mentioned by name. There was no indication he let them know where he lived when he did contact them.

To his family members The Elder must have been a missing person for at least those twenty-three years. He never wrote his name and never corrected the spelling of Sharky when others wrote it. People quietly questioned if his last name could have originally been spelled Sharkey, but there are no legal records to prove it one way or the other.

The Elder claimed that he was an Orthodox Jew from the lineage of Joseph and tribe of Judas. I never heard him speak Yiddish, yet he claimed he knew the language. He spoke English well and never seemed willing or interested in learning much Pennsylvania Dutch. He spoke a lot about the Nazi camps and the Jews escaping from Hitler. We wondered if it were possible that his family escaped Hitler's camps. He had the colony order a book entitled *The Black*

Book, Nazi Crime Against The Jewish People, published in 1946 by the Jewish Black Book Committee. He appeared obsessed with this book and the things that happened to the Jews, God's people.

How did The Elder know to go to Aberdeen, Mississippi? He always responded, "God led me to the Amish." Some colony members speculate that he might have heard from Amish relatives in Pennsylvania about the Aberdeen Amish who were in an unsettled state at that time. He might have read of this in *The Budget,* a paper published concerning the Amish and their activities. Others believed that while The Elder was in prison he might have met Amish men who refused to be involved in the military. In the early 1900s Amish fellows who refused to participate in the armed services were put in prison to serve their military time until the non-combatant laws went into effect. Perhaps The Elder served time in prison with some non-resistant Amish men and learned of them and their ways of living. The Elder said he didn't believe in the government and protested any military action, claiming to have been in Washington D.C. at the White House to protest the military draft. He indicated that some of his time in prison was for draft evasion.

The Elder maintained an air of mystery, speaking of his prison experiences on different occasions. He would stroke his chin and gray beard downward as he spoke. "In prison I once fasted for forty days and forty nights because they would not serve kosher food according to the Jewish tradition and my requests. During the depression I was picked up on the streets for vagrancy and curfew violations."

It remains unknown how many different times The Elder was in prison, how much of his prison time was for military resistance, or how much was for other offences. He never revealed whether he had committed any major crimes. Most of the time he appeared like a quiet, docile man.

"I learned much of the Bible while imprisoned," The Elder said, "and I know it cover to cover. I had a car and drove in my younger years, and I worked on the railroad. I knew more and worked harder and faster than anybody around me. I'm well traveled. I jumped on trains and rode coast to coast, and I hitchhiked much of my traveling years. At times I slept in cardboard boxes to stay warm. You need to know there were a lot of good homeless people. I was also an electrician in Pennsylvania, and I gave my mother all my checks. I stayed with her and took care of her till she died. During that time my brother, Bill, kept asking me if and when I was going to start running after women."

Some in our colony questioned if The Elder was a eunuch from birth or otherwise. That too remains a mystery. This man knew about sexuality but didn't show any personal interest.

Did he ever have a driver's license? Did he ever have a social security number, which he claimed not to believe in? I don't know.

Keith and Evangeline Bickerton, a couple from Pennsylvania, claimed to know Mack Sharky before he settled with the Amish. They had three small children Kenny, Mark, and Faith. The Elder agreed to let this family come live with the colony on a trial bases to see if they wanted to follow his teachings. The Bickerton's stayed only a short time and moved back to where they came from. Keith later became a preacher.

When The Elder first came to Aberdeen, he made it very clear that he believed in keeping the Golden Rule. Initially that was the only rule he taught, but he soon added the Ten Commandments. Before long he added the dietary laws to his growing list of rules. He even let the Amish people know that if they wanted to be assured of God's acceptance he expected them to sell all their pigs and obey his "no pork" rules. In the Amish community The Elder became known as the Sabbath keeper, a self-acclaimed secret man that could not marry because of his Nazarite position, and a man that learned the Bible well and held strong opinions.

The first five or six years in Lael Colony The Elder occasionally liked to ride to town with the men to get groceries, but he stayed in the truck and waited. On one trip with Abraham Schrock, The Elder's right hand man, something under the truck went wrong. According to

Abraham he stopped the truck and crawled under it to find the problem. Peering out from under the truck he saw The Elder in his black shoes slowly pacing back and forth alongside the truck fearing somebody might come, stop to help, and see him.

"I can quickly fix the truck with a wrench if you'll give me that wrench on the floor of the cab," Abraham shouted.

"No! I can't do that. I'm a servant of God and can only do God's work," the Elder answered. "I can't pick up a wrench."

"You don't have to pick up the wrench. Just push it out of the cab and then kick it under here where I can reach it." Abraham waited for an answer.

"No! No! That's not the kind of work for a holy man of God," The Elder replied.

Taking a moment to clear his thoughts, Abraham wrinkled his face and chose to humble himself. He crawled out from under the truck, picked up the wrench, and tossed it under the vehicle. Without a word he turned and picked up a cap in the truck and put it on his head.

"You look silly with that beaker cap on," The Elder calmly said.

Abraham quietly crawled under the truck and soon had it fixed and ready to go again. Returning to the cab he took the cap off and laid it behind the seat.

"From now on those worldly beak-type caps are banned," The Elder announced.

"The cap was given to me when I sold timber last week. I thought it would keep the dirt and grease off my head while under the truck," Abraham replied.

The Elder was unmoved. "You can burn that hat with the slabs and trash at the sawmill tomorrow. We won't wear those kinds of hats," The Elder ordered.

"What's wrong with the hat?"

"The hat's too much like worldly stuff. We are to be separated and different from the world. Godly!" Then The Elder uttered a very strange statement. "I'm hoping that God calls me to take Christ's place someday."

The ride home was a silent one. Abraham knew he dare not repeat what The Elder said and did on this trip or he would be made a fool, questioned, and doubted. Though he was confused by the actions he remained quiet when The Elder announced his new rule about the beaker hat.

The Elder didn't ride to town much after that incident. However his list of rules kept growing. When most of the colony had moved to Tennessee in 1951, The Elder allowed one last trip to the doctor for all the men and boys so they could be circumcised to prepare them for heaven. That proved to be an ordeal!

So did Grandma Miller's pregnancy with her last child, Benja. It was one year after The Elder declared there should be total celibacy. Grandma suffered horrible embarrassment with her sinful act in full view. She told Mom that she considered suicide and could hardly face anybody.

The winter of 1952 my mom followed another of The Elder's more bazaar orders. She stood at our wood stove and dropped her marriage license into the fire. Next she took the collection of pictures of her three children in her hands. With a stressed look she said, "Clarence, burning our children's baby pictures and birth certificates is hard to do."

"The servant of God ordered them burned," Dad growled.

Dropping the birth certificates into the stove Mom watched as they lay on a log and one by one began to burn. The pictures followed. In anguish she cried, "It's extremely hard to see the little footprints shriveling up and burning, and they'll never return."

The reflection in Mom's moist eyes showed fire but no rainbows. As I sat on the chair, I didn't understand what this was all about.

Then Mom dropped the last of our pictures into the stove, her one wedding photo, and a few of us children. Mom staring into the stove said, "Clarence, this is too much! The faces of our children are burning to ashes," Mom turned her head away and wiped her cheeks.

Mom stood tall as she turned deliberately from the stove.

"I didn't like doing it, but it all boils down to this: it's better than going to hell or having our children go to a fiery hell and burn like that. That would be much worse and much more fearful."

"Mary, we aren't to have past records of any kind or a likeness of God in picture form so you did the right thing. Don't worry about it. It's okay," Dad reassured.

"Clarence, I made myself do it just like he instructed. I had to! As The Elder said, 'you give up everything and follow God.' We'll give up anything. Anything! It's better giving up everything than it is to go to hell . . . even our children's pictures, our marriage license, or whatever. We must do anything to save our souls from hell," Mom sighed. As an after thought, "Even if the children get sick from fasting. Anything!" And she had alluded to another rule and its impact on us.

"It's okay. The children will get older and fasting won't be so hard on them. This was their first year. They're only three, four, and five. They're young now. They'll grow and handle it better later," he said.

Listening to this last part reminded me of the Day of Atonement. It was a day of fasting. There was to be neither food nor water throughout the day. During my first experience I suffered from dry heaves. In mid-afternoon we were allowed to put water in our mouths and swish it around before spitting it out, but our parents watched to be sure we didn't swallow any. This caused my dry heaves to worsen. The day after Atonement Day I still felt sick from the 24 hour fast without food or water. If I ate, I vomited. It was a rainy day and I lay watching Mom sew on her treadle sewing machine making our clothes.

"Lois, just rest today and you will feel better tomorrow," Mom repeated.

The Elder's beliefs grew. His list of rules expanded with the passing of time, and he even changed some of his previous rules. His arrival, his teachings, and his list of dos and don'ts changed lives. His rules became the law.

The power of one man to totally control a group of

intelligent human beings was evident. No one foresaw the future.

Chapter 6

Isolation

When we moved to Lael Valley, little did I, or my parents, know that our new home and promised land would force us to become totally isolated from the real world. At the age of four I had no clue that I would never again see my Grandma Long or any relatives from my dad's family who lived in Indiana. We didn't realize all family contacts outside Lael Colony would be stopped completely.

Only one secret post office box was established for the entire colony in Florence, Alabama. This was done to prevent anybody from finding our group. The address could not be given to any relatives or used by individual colony members. Two fathers were appointed to use Christian Amstutz's truck once a month to go pick up the colony mail and to buy needed groceries. There would be no newspapers, no radios or televisions, and no way of knowing what happened in the world beyond the oak boundaries of our 2,000 plus acres.

"Let there be peace here in this valley," The Elder ordered. "Be thankful! We have escaped the heathen world and all the evil people in it."

We were isolated from the outside world, but I had other things to deal with.

I liked listening to Mom and Grandma talk Dutch, and I thought sentences in Dutch. I would ask Mom what some words meant if I felt unsure. She told me each time and added, "When will you stop asking so many questions and saying 'why'? You are more of a 'why child' than any child I have ever heard. Do you need to know everything?"

After hearing those words enough times, it made me

start holding back some of my questions. I learned to wait, watch, and listen to find my own answers in time.

One day as we visited Grandma, Joseph Amstutz went past her house on the sawmill tractor with the throttle wide open and thud! The tractor ran over our Teddy and killed him as we watched. Our tiny, brown, fluffy friend we liked so much, cuddled in bed and on our trip to the valley, instantly lay dead before our eyes. Teddy was gone forever, and we were not allowed to buy another dog. This saddened us greatly and even though we were not to cry, tears welled in my eyes and tracked down my cheeks.

"No! No! No! You don't cry," Mom ordered.

"*Sham dich von do hila!* (Shame on you if you cry!)" Grandma said. "That's disobeying your mother. You're a big girl now and not a baby. *Nay, do moust net hila.* (No, you must not cry.) You can enjoy Trixie."

He was Grandma's and Grandpa's white Spitz dog that I enjoyed until a rattlesnake bit him. I felt sad when Trixie's paw swelled up and he died. This served as a warning of what could happen to us if we were bitten by a snake.

"These snakes are the Devil working among us. Be careful and don't let that Devil ride your backs and cause you to do evil," The Elder warned. "Nobody buy another dog! For the Bible says in Deuteronomy 23:18 not to because it's an abomination unto the Lord thy God," he ordered.

We were positive Deuteronomy 23:18 did not have anything to do with dogs and Lael Colony.

The Elder was isolated from common sense and Biblical accuracy!

After that Grandma and Grandpa's cat, Tiger, usually had my attention at Grandma's when we weren't busy working. One day when Mom took Fred, Joan, and me to visit Grandma, Fred and I helped Enos and Besodeiah rack up freshly split firewood to dry. This wood was split into 2x2x14 inch pieces for their kitchen stove. When Mom or Grandma weren't looking and Joan thought she could get away with it, she would kick over our racks of hard work. She was having fun pulling these pranks, but we were afraid if The Elder happened to stop by he would consider it play and that was wrong.

We were isolated from childish play!

We had to be careful in Grandma's backyard when we went to their *hizeley* (outhouse) because Marlow, their reddish brown billy goat, would chase us. Once I ran to the *hizeley* and Marlow came charging behind me. I barely made it to the door and popped inside before he was at the door snorting and throwing his big head, racked with two giant horns. My heart pounded. I wondered, *What would have happened to me if I hadn't out run him?*

Once ready to leave I peeked out a tiny nail hole to see if Marlow had left or was far enough away that I felt I could run to the house before he could get to me. When I opened the *hizeley* door and set my feet on the ground, my heart raced faster than my feet. I ran for the house and popped in the back door before Marlow caught up with me. Marlow stood outside the back door for awhile before walking away to guard the nanny goats in the backyard. He didn't bother us in the front yard, so we stayed there while Mom and Grandma talked.

We were isolated from modern conveniences.

Mom and Grandma sat on logs visiting. Benja, age two, sat on Grandma's lap or stayed near her until he took a nap on a pallet comforter.

"Mary, there are some hard things to get used to. Before we moved from Hamilton, The Elder told us to use flour sacks with small flowery prints to make the girls and ladies dresses," Grandma said. "He said, 'It's different than the Amish clothes and okay with God to wear printed or plain clothes.' The flower prints seemed *veltlich* (worldly) to me. But this saved on the cost of dress material as the little girls outgrew their dresses. The older girls enjoyed making your younger sisters new light colored dresses with small flower prints. I choose not to wear *zierote* (ornamental) dresses, even if it was okay with God. I sure didn't want to be in the red (meaning bad.) I wanted to stay in the clear (meaning good.)

"Then suddenly one day The Elder said, 'Don't make

any more clothes from printed flour sacks. You shouldn't be proud of your clothing, yourself, or anything. Only use the plain colored flour sacks. Dye all your flowery dresses black or navy blue to cover up the flowers. I'll design some plain colored clothes different from the Amish, Jews, or anybody else's clothes.' Then he appointed Martha to make patterns, cut the material, and sew the garments as he instructed. Sometimes things just don't make sense."

We were isolated from consistency.

"After we came to Tennessee, The Elder assigned the girls partners," Grandma said one afternoon when she and Mom were visiting. "They aren't to go anyplace without their appointed partner. It's to be for their good, but some personalities grind. Some of the girls naturally gravitated together and are now split up and must go with another sister against their natural grain and will. That's hard for some."

"Why do they need partners?" Mom asked.

"I guess if one gets hurt or in trouble there's still help, and that's safe."

"Oh look, here come Polly and Martha," Mom interrupted. "I can't believe The Elder paired those two sisters of mine together. Polly is only 10-years-old, and Martha's twenty."

"*Mich ouch!* (Me too.) *Ich vonna vos sie vella.* (I wonder what they want,)" Grandma said.

"We're to get more matches," Polly blurted. "*Maoude, gook!* (Mary, look!) See my new dress? It had yellow flowers, and I liked it. It was pretty and made me feel good, but now it's all dyed black." There was a hint of childish disappointment — as much as she dared show.

"Polly, your dress still looks good," Mom consoled. "I dyed some of Lois' and Joan's dresses like that too."

While Polly continued talking, Martha dashed in the house for matches.

Darting from the house she said, "We need to hurry back to the sawmill. They want these matches to burn slats." She signaled for Polly to come, and they rushed off.

After the pair left the discussion returned to the Elder's clothing rules.

"Polly really got upset the last time you came to Hamilton to visit us because The Elder had instructed us not to wear any printed flour sack dresses around you and your family. It was right after his instructions to dye all of them, and we didn't have them all dyed yet. Polly was given a blue dress with a print to wear, and she had a fit. She was sure we were disobeying The Elder," Grandma said. "I think we found another girl's dress for her to wear until we dyed all of hers. Then the older girls let Polly pick out a plain color material to make Joan a dress, and she picked yellow. Kay picked aqua for Lois, and *Quaudy* picked blue for a shirt for Fred. The children enjoyed making the grandchildren's clothes. I don't know why The Elder ever let us wear those kinds of colors and prints and then he said we couldn't. Maybe the children got too excited over their clothes, and he quickly stopped it. I'm satisfied if we stay with a couple darker colors."

We were isolated from beautiful colors!

"I was surprised the other day when Fred wore his dark, plain-colored, sweater-type jacket. When The Elder saw him he looked close at the back of his jacket and said, 'That's got to go. We can't have that ram with horns on his jacket. Dye it!' So I dyed the jacket the next day," Mom said. "The logo was so small I didn't give it much thought. I didn't think it mattered."

"I guess it does," Grandma said.

We were even isolated from designs!

Another time when we were visiting with Grandma the subject of clothes came up again, as it often did. Hearing a familiar voice, we all looked up when Grandma announced, "Oh, here comes Martha. She'll explain The Elder's clothing instructions. Martha knows! She has worked hard under The Elder's instructions to make the newly designed clothes."

Martha began a detailed account of our future wardrobes. "The girls and ladies will soon wear The Elder's newly designed colony dresses and clothes. The dresses will have a uniform look – floor length, heavy twill, and pilgrim gray. It will be a tube-like jumper style designed to conceal any shape. Two-inch wide matching straps will cross suspender-like in back to hold the dress up."

Mom was listening very closely as Martha continued, "Four flat layers of navy blue fabric surrounding the bottom will serve as weights to keep the wind from blowing the skirt. These extra four fabric layers must extend twelve inches up from the skirt bottom. An extra eight-inch panel with three stays is sewn inside the skirt front to prevent the skirt from blowing in between the legs or dipping in between them when sitting down."

Mom looked at Grandma. There was nothing she could say.

Martha took a deep breath and looked at Grandma before she started again. "There are to be two light blue, one-inch wide stripes circling the bust line of the jumper. I don't know what those are for, but The Elder included them in his design. Both dress sides have inserted deep pockets, and below the pockets are large pleats to allow for longer steps. On the left side above the pocket running to the jumper bust line is a seven-inch zipper with an inside button. Sewed inside the jumper is a seven-inch waistband to help absorb some of the dress weight off the shoulders. The Elder insisted that I make a secret pocket inside the dress.

"I made the patterns and cut the material. Naomi helped me sew the dress, and Ruby modeled the dress for The Elder and us. The Elder ordered that we make Naomi's dresses black instead of gray. I don't know why. She is the only lady in the colony who has to wear a black dress. I think it will make her feel like a black sheep."

I could tell Mom was unhappy with all the details, but she didn't say anything. She could tell Martha was not finished.

"Under the jumper a long-sleeved white blouse must be worn." Martha began talking faster like she wanted to finish while Mom and Grandma were still listening. "The blouse's collar, button front, bottom and four-inch button cuffs are trimmed with blue ribbon as a reminder to keep God's commandments. Coats are navy blue and also trimmed with blue ribbon. Ladies uncut hair will be braided, pinned up, and hidden under pilgrim gray, twill head coverings matching the dress. Unlike Amish head coverings these coverings have a tail. Blue or gray head scarves can be worn over the gray covering and tied under the chin. On the Sabbath and special occasions larger white headscarves worn over the covering are to be pinned under the chin — to cover the bodice and give a shawl look. Floor length slips with short sleeves will be worn and under pants will be floor length like pajama bottoms. Bras must be made to flatten and be very tight. The ladies will wear dark navy blue socks and tennis shoes."

Martha let out a deep sigh. Mom looked at Grandma, and we all relaxed. I didn't understand all she had explained, but I could tell it must be hard to make all those clothes.

We were not only isolated from style, we were isolated from comfort!

Grandma looked directly at Martha. "That is thorough enough! Now what about the men?"

Martha knew the answer. "Men will wear long-sleeved, heavy twill work shirts, denim coveralls or pants — no *latz hussa* (flop pants) without zippers like Amish wear. They will also wear long-handled long-johns with the button front and back. They will wear the same clothes year around. Men will wear leather work shoes. As usual, fathers will wear felt hats on the Sabbath and boys straw hats, and they all will wear straw hats for everyday. Men's beards will remain untrimmed and hair cut short unlike Amish."

"Humph!" was all Grandma had to say. The tedious details about The Elder's design for our clothes were almost too much to endure. After a long pause Grandma changed the subject.

"*Ech fashta net favos des* (I don't understand why this) The Elder picked Martha as a special older girl in our family, and he gave her a middle name — San, which means saint in Hebrew. Now we are supposed to always call her Martha

San. Then he picked *yuscht ain glani matlie* (just one little girl) from four different families to be special. He picked Polly in our family. The other girls are Susanna Amstutz, Barbara Schrock, and Becky Miller. These girls are all about age ten and are to see who can do the best. I guess he plans to judge them or God will tell him who does the best. It makes Polly try harder to work and be good. I don't know why The Elder didn't change their names or give them middle names."

"If it helps them be good, I guess it's good," Mom responded.

I knew I wanted to be good and stay in the clear like Grandma because if I was bad and in the red they said God would write it in my record book in heaven. I felt sure God wrote my name in His big record book once for stealing candy, and I had a bad flaw written in my heavenly record book. *God's record books in heaven must be huge to write every person's record in it,* I thought.

As a child, I soon learned my first lesson about stealing or taking something that didn't belong to me. Grandpa had gone to town with Christian Amstutz to purchase The Elder's special ordered candy. Grandpa also bought a bag of candy for his family. They seldom had candy and when they did they always divided it up between all fifteen in their family so each person had the same amount. Besodeiah had his few pieces at the woodpile atop a block of wood. I saw his candy. It was the first candy I'd seen since we left Indiana and it tempted me.

The candy looked especially good since my dad didn't allow me to have candy because of my toothaches. I waited till everybody turned their backs and walked toward the house for lunch. Then I took only one piece of Besodeiah's candy and stuffed it in my pocket. I ran and caught up with them. I instantly felt guilty for taking the candy. My conscience bothered me. I felt convicted and certain it was not worth having candy and a guilty conscience. *I will return Besodeiah's candy after lunch when we go back out to work,* I thought.

After lunch the boys beat me to the woodpile. I went

with Mom and Grandma and there were too many eyes watching, and I couldn't return the candy without being seen. Time came for us to quit stacking wood, and I still had Besodeiah's candy in my pocket as we walked away. I felt guilty and feared that Mom or somebody would find it, and the punishment would be severe — standing at least a half or whole day with my nose in a corner of our living room. I disposed of the candy as we walked home. First I popped it in my mouth for a quick taste. I was afraid somebody would see me chew so I trailed behind and took the candy out of my mouth and threw it like a rock deep into the woods. I asked God to forgive me for breaking one of the Ten Commandments by stealing, but I didn't forgive myself for such a sinful act. Later I confessed. "Besodeiah, I'm in the red because I took a piece of your candy when we worked on the woodpile. Will you forgive me for taking your candy?"

"Yes, I forgive you," he said. "I don't like candy and would have given it to you if you had asked. I never missed that candy."

The candy wasn't worth the feeling of having a bad conscience, and I never stole anything again. I learned that God convicts children when they do wrong, even at a young age.

On chicken canning day families gathered between our house and Grandpa's at Swanegan Creek. We worked near the spring where a wire cage was kept under water to keep our fresh milk, hand churned butter, and other foods cold. The cage held our food from washing away. Grandpa's family and ours shared this spring and cage. Other families had springs with cages closer to their homes.

On canning day I helped carry water from the creek to fill the huge, black, wash pots and the many round silver tubs. I helped pick up twigs and wood to start a fire under the kettles. Meanwhile, chickens were hung up by their legs all spaced apart in rows on long clothesline type ropes; their heads were slashed off with a sharp butcher knife. They were quickly dipped into the boiling wash pots and their feathers plucked. Then they were washed, cut up in pieces, and put

73

into canning jars. I helped in the plucking section of the production line. I remember this big chicken-canning workday as fun work. However, I didn't like the chickens being killed.

At the end of the day during clean up around the creek, my brother and other boys caught poisonous snakes bare-handed. They held their fingers tightly behind the snakes' heads to prevent getting bitten. I never wanted to take part in that risky challenge. They became skilled snake killers to protect us from harm. Snakes were the only living creatures not used for food that the Elder gave us permission to kill. He claimed all birds were good signs and snakes were evil signs and of the Devil. We were not to kill anything else, including bugs, because the Bible says in Exodus 20:13, "Thou shalt not kill."

Almost every afternoon Mom asked, "Whose turn is it to gather this day's eggs? How many do you think the hens laid today?"

Out the door we all went scrambling through the back yard, past the outhouse, and into the hen house. We counted each egg as the gatherer carefully collected them. We noticed the different sizes, shapes, and colors of light and dark brown eggs. We took caution not to break any eggs because it could cost us our next breakfast.

Dad would return home from the sawmill or the west hill after cutting timber all day. Mom fixed pancakes for supper, and we were in bed by dark. The next morning we ate scrambled eggs with fresh biscuits and washed it down with goat's milk. Then Dad left to work at the sawmill.

Mom knew how to make work sound exciting. "Who wants the privilege of helping make lye soap today?"

We all responded. "I do!"

"Go gather *schtecka* (sticks) to start a fire under the wash pot," Mom ordered.

We all scrambled off to the woods fetching an arm full of dry twigs as Mom gathered the ingredients together. This work lasted most of the day. We enjoyed making lye soap and seeing the fruit of our hard work. I liked watching Mom cut the soap into bars. It was a treat to wash our dirty hands with our own homemade soap. Sometimes others in the colony came to help us.

Mom always planned our busy wash day every Sunday. After resting all day Saturday — our Sabbath — we blazed with energy and were ready to help. We gathered sticks in the woods to start the fire under our big, black wash pot. To fill the pot we helped carry water from the creek halfway up the eastside of our backyard. Mom used two-gallon buckets with a wire bail. "You children use those small metal molasses buckets to help. If they are too heavy, only make them half full," Mom instructed.

With a five foot long poking stick — a skinned two-inch oak tree — Mom always poked and stirred the clothes in the boiling water. She fished them out with the stick and finished washing and rinsing them in big silver wash tubs.

"Lois, bring that milking stool to this tub and stand on it to scrub these smaller pieces of clothing," Mom ordered.

Wosh! Wosh! Wosh! "Ouch! I just slipped and took the skin off two fingers," I said shaking some blood from my fingers.

"When you are done scrubbing that bunch of clothes, go in the house and get the white tape, scissors, and a worn-out garment from the rag box, and I will wrap your fingers if they're still bleeding," Mom said. "Keep your eyes on your work and be careful so that won't happen again." I learned fast how vicious our old, ribbed wash-board could be when I put all my might into working hard.

"Fred come! It's your turn to work on the ringer," Mom called. We alternated turning the handle on the ringer to press all the water out of our clothes. "Slow down a bit . . . now turn the handle backwards. We can get that dress through. Here, I'll loosen the tension for these bigger pieces." We soon learned how quickly fingers could get pinched in the ringer while feeding clothes in between the rollers.

"Lois, shake the wrinkles out of the clothes in the basket and hand them to Fred. Fred, you hand them to me. You two keep up with me as I hang them on the lines."

Our backyard soon became a wall of clothes waiting for the sun to rise above the treetops and to get what little breeze might stir to dry them.

Toward evening Mom issued another directive. "You children line up at the clothesline to carry clothes in the house. I will load your arms with clothes. Carry the load into the house and hurry back out and get in line for another load."

Wash day was a busy day without any of today's modern conveniences.

In the spring we spent hours helping Mom in the garden picking up rocks and stones. We admired their beautiful colors, some even mosaic. Fred and I wanted to put the pretty ones in our *socha* (pockets) and save them, but we could not keep any as precious stones. We had to haul all of them to the woods and dump them on the rock pile. We tried laying some nice colors and shaped stones to the side to view them again, but they always came up missing. Our joyful treat at the end of the day was throwing small stones or dirt chunks in the air and watching bats swoop down and try to catch them, until they became wise to us tricking them.

The next day Mom said, "I will make trenches. Lois, put the okra seed this far apart in the trench," she said holding up spaced fingers. "Then I will cover them up. Fred, you drop beans in this row."

After a few days we had our garden planted. Soon we pulled weeds and grass, and the task never seemed to end. We also helped harvest vegetables, wash them, and prepare them for canning.

"Lois, add a half teaspoon of salt to each quart jar," Mom would say. She did most of the canning until we were older. We enjoyed eating the crops and were reminded that it was because of our hard work and God's blessings that we had the good food.

Often in the summer after working in the garden, Mom took her dirty children, a bar of soap, and a washcloth to the creek swimming hole to get them ready for bed. We returned clean before suppertime. One time I remember going to the creek for a bath just before dusk. I felt tired and dirty but happy. That night Mom seemed in a hurry. It was a known fact that I feared having my face in the water, after I nearly drowned in Lake Michigan as a small child.

"Fred, you're first. Come on into the creek with me," Mom ordered.

She always took us into the creek with our underwear on, and we came out with it still on. We never had swimsuits. After she bathed us we went to the creek bank, grabbed a towel, and dried off. While wrapped in the towel, we slipped out of our wet underwear and into dry nightclothes.

"Lois, it's your turn now. Come into the water with me," Mom commanded.

She quickly dipped the washcloth in the water and then straight to my face. I flinched and my hands went to my face. Without a word Mom instantly grabbed my braid, put her other hand on my head, and shoved it under water. I struggled fearfully, panicked, and gulped in water. I felt as if I would drown before I could get to the surface to breathe again. Once my head was out of the water I began crying.

"That'll teach you not to put your hands in your face when I want to wash it," Mom snapped. "If you cry, you'll go under again. If you put your hands even near your face, you'll go under again. If I hear a peep out of you, you're going under water!"

I coughed and coughed as quietly as possible and shook as if I had Parkinsons disease.

"Get on the creek bank, Lois, dry off, and get your nightgown on. I better not hear a word out of your mouth," Mom growled.

I felt weak as I walked to the creek bank. I dried off, slipped on my long nightgown, and out of the wet underwear.

My feelings were crushed to think that my mom had deliberately nearly drowned me. This was the third time I felt like I was drowning. The first time was at Lake Michigan when I tried to walk on a bunch of lily pads, a surface that looked so solid at the end of the pier. My parents stood near the pier talking and didn't notice that I had fallen into the lake. I knew nothing about swimming.

I fought fiercely. Unexpectedly I would surface, start to breathe, and then go under again taking lots of water into my lungs. I didn't feel I would make it to the surface for one last bob up in the cold water. I floated aimlessly feeling exhausted, limp, and hopeless as I drifted under water. Suddenly when I surfaced the fourth time, my dad grabbed me. When I coughed, I coughed water from my lungs. I was very young, but I can remember this as if it happened yesterday. I knew my dad had just pulled me out in the nick of time, and he surely saved my life. I cried back then, and they wrapped me in a blanket. Now things were different.

The second time I experienced a drowning sensation occurred when a full glass of water was tossed in my face. I gasped and breathed in the water. I cried, and coughed, and went to my mom for comfort, but I couldn't this time.

This third time I walked home from the creek extremely hurt and disappointed to know that my mom would do that to me in her rush and frustration. Mom and Joan trailed behind. Fred and I walked ahead going home.

"Mom almost drowned me," I whispered still trembling and teeth chattering.

"I know," Fred agreed as he looked at me with big, scared eyes. "Are you going to be okay?" He lowered his head and looked at our footsteps as we walked down that dirt road side by side.

My heart ached to think that my mom had nearly drowned me. Alone! I lay in my bed quiet, feeling humble and helpless. I heart-cried for a long time. The only comfort I felt was knowing that God cared about me. As I listened to the whippoorwills outside singing on that dark night, I finally went to sleep.

I learned to know all the people in the colony by their first names. I enjoyed being around them and working with them. We walked through the woods, across creeks, and on logging roads to visit other families and friends. And they came to visit us. I liked everybody in the colony, but something was seriously wrong.

I was told not to think about Grandma Long because

she was a worldly bad person, an un-repented gentile that would burn in hell someday. I was told that's why I had to be as good as possible — perfect — so I would never go to hell like her and all the rest of the people in the world outside our colony.

We were isolated from all of Dad's family!

Patricia Hochstetler

Chapter 7

Reality

Was this really utopia?

The people of Lael Colony seemed quite settled, compliant, and committed after seven years as a colony. They accepted life as God allowed it and enjoyed His blessings on this promised land. Our Sabbath meetings were held from 1-5 P.M. in homes, in our schoolhouse, and occasionally outdoors if The Elder decided, weather permitting.

The Elder's orders were very detailed and definitely uncompromising.

"There shall be no complaining in our streets or dirt roads as the children of Israel did," The Elder commanded. Placing his left arm across his waistline, he propped his right elbow on his left hand, put his right index finger on his lips, and then began stroking each side of his mustache over and over. Pausing and stroking his beard, The Elder added, "Children, be sure you all have learned Ephesians 6:1-3." Then he softly quoted, "Children, obey your parents."

"Adults, obey God and make sure you memorize The Golden Rule, The Ten Commandments, and know The Dietary Laws. Make sure everybody learns all the books in the Bible. We will have *Bible book hunts* to see who can find the places the fastest. We will have hunts for a book and a chapter and hunts for book, chapter, and verse. Learn the books, drill each other on them, and practice finding them fast."

Sometimes The Elder had group walks for those who wanted to go, and he even had orders for them. We walked to the top of the west hill or to the north or east gates. The

Elder led as we started the walks, and everybody was to walk at his pace. If he walked briskly, we must hurry to keep up. If he walked slowly, everybody adjusted to his pace. Once we reached his chosen destination, The Elder barked the next order, "Everybody stop and stand still. Do an about face and stand for a moment. Keep your assigned spots and don't look back. You know what happened to Lot's wife in the Bible when she looked back." I guess he thought we didn't remember for he always added, "She turned to a pillar of salt."

Without even a few moments to enjoy the beauty of the area The Elder commanded, "Walk forward."

This type of turning around put The Elder at the tail end of the group, and he stayed there until he decided to gradually pass to the right of the crowd. He slowly eased around each row of people, usually three or four people per row. He was selective about those with whom he spoke. Some he totally ignored. Before the group arrived at the spot where they had started, The Elder always managed to be leading them.

"When we go on these walks, I'm always bothered that The Elder lets my son, Rudy, go out of line and walk beside him," Abraham Schrock commented one day. "He never lets anybody else do that. I wanted to make Rudy get back in line, but The Elder would always address me firmly, 'Rudy is all right here.' So I couldn't say anything more. It just didn't seem right. Rudy was very intelligent, and he became almost obsessed with being right at The Elder's side all the time. It looked like Rudy wanted to be just like The Elder and took great joy in leading the people. It seemed Rudy ran out where angels would fear to walk."

Most people found these walks fun and interesting because they didn't have to stay home and rest all day on the Sabbath. The walks seemed to reinforce The Elder's admonition to the people: "follow God and take the narrow path and not the devil's broad path that leads to destruction."

It was only a matter of time until another rule was added to the growing list. The Elder announced, "You now follow well and walk in lines and in an orderly fashion. From this time on you must walk to our Sabbath meetings in a more orderly manner. You have shown me you can do it, so walk as I tell you."

It is difficult to understand how grown men and women would listen to such details and follow them. It was as if they were all under a spell of a dictatorial drill sergeant.

"The men shall walk ahead according to age, the oldest first. And the women will walk behind the men from the oldest to the youngest."

The Elder claimed this formation would help parents control their children, and each child had an appointed place to walk. Fear was the controlling factor.

"If any of you think you have sinned, fast a day or two, and ask God to forgive you. You have all done well observing the Day of Atonement," The Elder announced. "Now I want you to keep the Feast of Tabernacles and the Passover. Unlike the worldly Jews, we will keep the Passover in the fall and the Feast of Tabernacles in the spring. I will go by the moon and count the days and tell you when and which days to observe. They will begin and end with a Sabbath. Sometimes there will be double Sabbaths when they begin or end near a regular Sabbath. This observance will last a week to ten days each."

The pronounced changes in the seasons for observing the feasts may have upset more than one person, but 20-year old Joseph Amstutz could not remain silent. He spoke to a friend, "David, I know the Passover is in the spring around Easter. We learned that in the public school. I don't know why The Elder is doing this!"

The Elder had done everything possible to keep Joseph Amstutz hidden from the public until now.

No one else publicly challenged The Elder, and he continued with his new calendar and doctrines. "While you are observing The Passover and Feast of Tabernacles, you will have plenty of time to study the Bible. Everybody should learn all the chapter headings in the Bible so you can quickly find anything you want. The young children should learn them all before they are eleven. We will call the Bible chapter headings 'the scripture lines' so nobody else knows what we mean. I will make a *Scripture Line* book for you.

"It would also be good to learn one Bible verse a day and say it at the table in the evening before supper right after the Bible chapter is read. I gave you fathers a floor prayer to say when you kneel and pray before your scripture reading at the table and a table prayer to say before you eat your meals. I will give each child age eight and older their own prayer to say at night before going to bed.

"Children, obey your parents and work hard to memorize your prayer and say it every night before you go to bed. Always pray in secret to the Lord Thy God. Go in a closet or secret place to pray your prayers. Parents, make sure your children obey and always keep them busy. That is to be done even if you need to make them move a woodpile from one place to another and back. Never allow idle hands."

"This is my prayer that The Elder gave me," Polly Miller told us. "Unto Thee, Lord God, I do pray. May my effort to seek Thy kindness by devotion be acceptable to Thee. I pray let Thy word be given me that it may be my hope and guide."

Another example of The Elder's prayer for a child was a bit more suitable to the child's age. "I pray may Thy peace be with me. I do want to try and please Thee, and live and praise Thee, and give Thee thanks daily. In Jesus name, Oh Lord, I pray, please help me."

There was no effort to make the prayer understandable to the child or to the parent. The children were expected to read their prayers from the paper The Elder had given them until they had them memorized. Prayer was a dutiful ritual established by The Elder.

He ordered that his dictated prayers be said by each person. He set no age or circumstance when we could pray our own personal prayers. No one dared question him.

By this time my family had settled into a daily and weekly routine. Our new house felt like home, and Lael Valley felt like our village with family and friends all around. At age five I was happy. I had learned Psalm 23 and Ephesians

6:1-3. I was trying hard to learn the Bible chapter headings, which The Elder called scripture lines, before I turned eleven. Mom and Dad were also trying to learn Bible verses and the scripture lines.

Dad worked hard every day with David and *Zaquaudus* (Zacharias) Miller. (We always called him Quaudy.) They were Mom's two oldest brothers.

One evening I overheard Dad telling Mom, "Mary, I enjoy working with your teenage brothers and watching them work together. I'm learning some Dutch words from them, especially *net so do* (don't do that.) They say it to each other so seriously that it tickles me. They think I sound weird when I try to say Dutch words. Some words they say sound pretty weird to me." Mom smiled, understanding Dad's struggle with the Pennsylvania Dutch.

The next day Dad came home quite upset. He had worked on the west hill cutting timber all day. "What's the problem?" Mom asked. His attitude had changed so drastically in just one day.

"The Elder sent word with Willie Miller for me to come in for a consultation with him tomorrow, and I don't know why. I'll go the first thing in the morning to see what he wants."

One look at Dad revealed his frustration. All they could do now was wait. The next morning Dad was still nervous when he went to meet with The Elder.

"Clarence, I heard you talking loud when you cut timber on the west hill yesterday," The Elder started. "You don't need to yell. Be quiet! Remember that silence is golden. You must also understand there will be no laughing. That's foolishness."

The scolding from The Elder made Dad angry, yet he dared not show it. No talking loud enough to be heard in the woods? No laughing? This was too much for him. After the meeting with The Elder Dad still tried to enjoy working with David and Quaudy and continued to learn Dutch words and phrases from them, but even that didn't help to sooth his growing frustration.

The summers were very hot. Little breeze circulated down in this moist valley. On top of the hills the wind could be felt, but that was a long way up. One morning when the sun rays showed and the white streaks looked like rain against the forest Grandpa said, "That's rain going up to the sun."

I gave him a quizzical look. "Yes, rain goes up, Lois. Did you know that?"

"No, Grandpa, rain comes down, not up"

"Look! See it right there. The sun is pulling the rain up out of the ground."

Confused, I looked closely. *Does rain really go up? I don't believe so. It rains from the clouds up in the sky not the ground below my feet. I'll see when it rains again.* The next time it rained I carefully watched the raindrops, and they were all coming down. I felt convinced that Grandpa was wrong, so I asked Mom, "Do you think it rains up or down?"

Having heard Grandpa's words earlier, Mom answered carefully, "The rain comes down from the clouds, and when the sun dries up the water and moisture, it looks like rain going up to the sun." I felt satisfied with her answer. Maybe Grandpa was half-way right!

Even with rain the ground remained so rocky that gardens and crops didn't do well. Food and money ran short. The hard work at the sawmill didn't produce enough income to support all the people. A change was inevitable.

Toward the end of summer The Elder ordered the fathers and most of the older children to go to the Mississippi Delta to pick cotton for six weeks. He ordered my Dad to go with Grandpa Miller and nine of his older children. Mothers stayed in the valley with the smaller children, the boys in their late teens, and The Elder. Uncle David, age seventeen, stayed because he was close to draft age and The Elder did not want any outsiders to see him and ask questions about any colony boys entering the military.

Mom and her brother, Uncle David, took Fred, Joan, and me with them to the top of the west hill to pick corn. We became tired and weary of picking up and down the rows.

"If you want a rest, stay here at the end of the rows and

shuck this pile of corn while we make the next round. I want it all done when we return," Mom instructed.

Fred and I shucked the corn as fast as we could and made plans to climb trees. Fred was six and I was five. With a year of tree climbing experience we felt quite skilled. Standing on the west hilltop we could see over several lower distant hilltops and all the treetops in the valley where we lived. It was a spectacular view!

"Let's race climbing a tree," Fred challenged excitedly. "I will count and on three start climbing. Okay?"

"Okay. If I climb to the top of the highest tall skinny tree on this hill I think I can see Indiana where Grandma Long lives." I spotted the tallest perfect tree about 30 feet high.

"One, two, three," and Fred started climbing. He climbed quickly. "I win," he declared proudly.

"You won, but my tree is taller, and I'm climbing to the top to see Indiana."

Fred stopped to rest, perched near the top of his tree, and watched me. As I neared the top, my tree swayed. I kept climbing. Looking over the trees I shouted, "I think I can see Indiana many hill-tops away." About that time the tall skinny tree bent over like a rainbow, leaving me dangling in mid-air holding on for life.

Fred rushed down his tree while I struggled to pull myself back up. None of our ideas worked, and I felt worn out trying. The bounce in the bent tree kept me from pulling myself back up. There ten to twelve feet above the ground I hung!

"Drop to the ground. Come on, let go, and drop to the ground. It's not that far," Fred claimed reassuringly.

"No, it's a long way down there, and I can't let go. It will kill me when I hit the ground or at least break my legs."

"Come on, drop, and I'll try to catch you." Fred coaxed.

"No! I can't."

"What are you going to do then?"

"I don't know. My arms are getting terribly tired."

"I'll go get Mom and Uncle David," Fred blurted as he ran off into the cornfield.

87

"Joan," I called to her as she lay sleeping on our cornhusk pile. She didn't answer me. She was always scared to climb on anything. I closed my eyes while my head ached and my ears rang. *It seems I have been hanging here for an hour all alone. When will they ever come? I can't hang much longer. My hands and arms are numb and I can't feel them anymore. Am I going to plunge to the ground and die here?*

I heard the mules running and the wagon rattling giving me hope for relief. Uncle David pulled the team of horses under me and stopped the wagon below me. Standing atop a heap of corn ears, he reached up for my bare feet as Mom asked, "Why did you climb so high?"

"I wanted to see Indiana! I wanted to see where we came from," I moaned.

"Why weren't you shucking corn?" Mom questioned.

"We had it all done."

Once off that tree I cannot describe the magnitude of relief I felt accompanied by total exhaustion. This taught me never to climb to the top of any tree. We were more careful but still climbed trees to pick the tasty wild muscadine grapes for our snack. We "canned" the grapes on the spot until we became too full to eat anymore.

Once Fred climbed a tree on the rocky steep west hill in our barnyard and was picking grapes and throwing them to me when he fell from the tree onto rocks, knocking the wind out of him. This scared me, and I was sure he was dying when I saw him gasping for breath.

"Mom! Mom! Mom!" I shrieked. "Fred fell out of the tree, and he's hurt."

Mom immediately abandoned the goat she was milking and ran out of the barn. She picked Fred up and carried him to the house. Blood dripped from his head. I followed alongside in disbelief. "Will he be okay?" I asked over and over with each step to the house. "Mom, will he be all right?"

Mom hurried silently. I held the door open. She gently placed Fred on our bench couch. I saw him breathe, and then he talked. She washed blood from his hair and found a badly bruised spot on his head.

"He must have hit his head on a rock," Mom said. "You stay here with him, and I'll go finish milking the goats."

Fred went to sleep and wouldn't talk to me. I felt concerned and wanted him to answer me, but I let him rest. He had a sore head the next morning but seemed okay. After these experiences our climbing habits changed to less often and lower branches. We enjoyed colorful fall leaves and picking up acorns from the forest floor instead.

With Dad and most of the men gone, we weren't too concerned about The Elder's rules.

Fall came and Dad, along with the others, returned from picking cotton. We were glad to have them back home, and we listened when they told us how hard they had all worked picking cotton. We really enjoyed hearing about the few fun things they were able to do while away from the colony. While working they would have a race to see who could pick the most pounds of cotton and reach the end of the row first. Dad told about how he and Aunt Kay, who was only fourteen, had a pancake-eating contest, and she won.

Sometime later while he was working at the sawmill, a log slipped striking Quaudy Miller. He fell on a cant hook and bruised and injured his tailbone area. Quaudy was disabled for an extended period. The Elder acted like an authority about injuries too. He advised, "make an ointment and put it on the bruised areas."Quaudy was only fourteen when the accident happened. Sometimes he asked to be taken to the sawmill where he could lay and watch other colony members work. Since he wasn't allowed to see any doctor, Quaudy let my dad use some of the techniques he had learned in the U.S. Marines to work on putting his spine back in place. Quaudy eventually healed enough to help at the sawmill again.

A while after Quaudy was back working at the sawmill another accident happened. An axe slipped while Luke was splitting wood, and it cut his leg to the bone. This open wound seemed severe. Nevertheless The Elder did not relent on his "no doctor" rule. He stated, "If Luke is good and has enough faith, he will heal." We would have to wait to see.

One cloudy afternoon we went to visit Grandma. "*Kinna,* (Children,)* Grandpa bought apples the last time he went to town," she announced looking at me. She knew how much I liked apples — my candy substitute. "All of you children can have one for a snack. The apples are in a gunnysack under the stairway."

My younger uncles, aunts, and siblings rushed to the kitchen and under the dark stairway where each one fished for an apple. I lingered behind and listened as Grandma and Mom continued talking.

"I got a problem, Mary. Becky was doing a good job sweeping the floor, and Polly heard The Elder telling her, 'You are the hard worker.' Then The Elder turned to Polly and said, 'You keep trying hard.' Another time Polly heard The Elder say to Barbara Schrock, 'You're the good one.' To Susanna Amstutz, The Elder said, 'You've done the best.' Now Polly just can't accept that. She says, 'I'm not fast, I'm not good enough, I'm not the best, and I can't try any harder.' I don't know what to do with her." Grandma shook her head. "Sometimes I send her to the field to work with her father. She hates to go, but this makes her feel special. What should I do?"

I heard all that while I waited till last to get my apple. I felt around in that gunnysack. *Lots of big apples and lots of little apples.* I wondered *about the color of each apple and what they looked like.* I took a big one and walked to the living room where Mom, Grandma, and the rest of the children had gone. Grandma took one look at me and said, "How did you get such a big apple? You couldn't see in there. It's too dark."

"I felt it was big," I said as I walked away.

I overheard Grandma talking to Mom about my big apple. I knew we were not to be greedy and always want the biggest piece of food, the best, or the last bite of other things, but I never felt I was choosing something away from anybody else because I was the last to pick an apple. Listening to them talk I began feeling guilty that I had a big apple. I offered to get a smaller one, but Grandma said *nay.* I made up my mind right then that anytime I ever had a chance to choose anything for myself I would always take the smallest or ugliest. I didn't want to have any issues about what I chose or did. We ate our apples and then went outside in the front yard until we had to go home to milk our goats.

In our family Mom always had us children draw sticks from her hand to decide who had first choice for the largest piece of food or a turn to be first and many more things. If I won the longest stick too often, I saw her hold the sticks tight and allow others another choice. That didn't feel good or fair, yet I couldn't say a word. The day of the apple incident I made up my mind that wanting the best, largest, most, or being first would be over for me because I would always offer to take the smallest of anything, the least amount, and be last in everything. No need to draw sticks for me anymore. The sticks could be between my brother and sister for whatever they wanted, and I would take what was left. That felt better than feeling guilty! I soon found out that I was just as full after eating the small pieces as I was after eating a larger one, and it didn't matter if I went last on anything. I was satisfied with everything and nothing disappointed me. Well, most of the time. Of course that was a child's personal opinion.

We were always with Mom. Most of the time when she went outside, we had to be outside, and when she was inside, we were inside with her. One wash day Mom sent me into the house to get matches that she had forgotten. I always wanted to taste pure sugar and wasn't allowed sweet stuff so the temptation was great. While inside, I quickly grabbed the matches, then a spoon, and opened our five-gallon metal sugar can. I ate about three big spoonfuls of sugar.

I wiped off the spoon, put it back where it had been, and pushed the sugar can back in its place on the floor behind a curtain. Oh, that sugar tasted so good. I didn't feel like I was stealing because the sugar belonged to my family. However, I knew that my parents would disapprove of this if they knew it, so I felt guilty. I never did it again because my conscience bothered me.

Living in the colony had produced some truly high standards in my mind. I really wanted to be perfect as I was told. I wanted be good like Lois in the Bible. It must be the Devil tempting me, so I resisted my natural urges to get and do what I wanted. No more spoons of sugar for me!

When Mom milked goats, Fred and I pushed hay out of the haymow for her. Then he and Joan and I jumped on the hay. One day Joan caught her hair on a roll of barbed wire that hung on the wall. Grandpa Miller walked in as Fred and I were trying to untangle Joan's hair. He pulled out his *sochmessa* (pocketknife) and cut off a chunk of her hair to free her.

"Grandpa! The rules are not to cut girl's hair, and we never have until now! Why did you do that?" I asked in total awe. I knew the rules!

"What were you children doing to get in this kind of problem?" Then as his reddish-brown beard and mustache jiggled on his narrow face he explained, "I had to do the best I could. Cutting her hair was better than pulling it out of her head. Now watch what you do and remember no more horseplay or jumping around like little colts and fillies."

He went on to see Mom and seemed distressed while talking to her as she milked the goats. As he often did, he leaned back against the inside barn wall, pulled his one foot up under his behind, and sat on his heel as the sole of his shoe rested flat against the wall. Was his paradise crumbling or slipping away?

Later Mom talked to me about it. "Your Grandfather was terribly *mootlos* (low mood or discouraged) today. The Elder told him to pipe water from the creek up to his house without a pump. He knew this wouldn't work, but he couldn't dispute it. A mile north Abraham ran a pipe from a spring on the east hill down to his chicken house and they had water close and handy to the house, but their water ran down hill not up."

Grandpa returned at milking time the next day, "The Elder told me where to put a fence and how to dig the fence postholes on the west hill. The ground is nearly solid rock, and it didn't work." Grandpa snorted, throwing up his hands as if to surrender. "Well, I guess I better not make a big ado over small things. If The Elder doesn't know that I can't run water up hill without a pump, why should he know I can't drive postholes through rock? Oh well, he knows the Bible and God talks to him. I guess he's a spiritual man, and I'm carnal. Maybe this is a test for me. I better go home and be quiet." He walked out silently.

Grandpa knew he dared not say a word to The Elder or anyone else that he felt he couldn't fulfill orders from a divine being. He seemed extremely disturbed over it as he left our place.

Our barn stood at the foot of the huge west hill and across the dirt road from our house. After watching Mom milk goats many times, like often before I begged, "Can I help milk?"

"No, not this time," Mom said in her rush to finish. I helped her clean things up and carry stuff to the house. The next day I decided to head for the barn alone and try milking a goat. I opened the gate and put feed in the trough. Our goat, Sandy, ran in, jumped up on the raised milking platform, and began eating. I quickly shut the headlock bar, hurried around to her udder with a milk pail, and tried my hand at milking.

"Sandy, stand still! I'm milking you," I commanded. "Don't! You just kicked my bucket over and dumped the milk and got dirt in it. Now stand still. And don't kick anymore. Am I squeezing too hard? I'll be careful."

My milking ability developed and milk covered the bottom of the bucket. I felt I had mastered goat milking. When I looked up, Mom stood in the door watching me. "What are you doing?"

"I'm milking a goat for you."

"Okay, you tried it. Now let Sandy go and don't do that again. We need the milk to drink, and you have dirt in it. That is wasteful."

I felt guilty, but after that Mom sometimes let me help her milk just a little bit. More often at milking time she sent my brother, sister, and me to pick green brier leaves — one of the goats' favorites — that we fed them leaf by leaf. This evening entertainment lasted for hours after milking and was a great joy picking leaves outside the fence where the goats couldn't reach. This made me feel like a big helper. It seemed that Fred helped more by defending us from snakes. For me snakes always remained leery creatures to deal with. Whenever I saw a snake around the barn or picking brier leaves, I called Fred and he tried to protect us.

I remember when Mom's first cousin, Lovina Schrock, came to help Mom in our garden. I followed Lovina around and carried the bucket as she harvested okra and picked other vegetables. We weeded our garden together. I thought she was an extremely nice, kind, and a mild natured person. She was nineteen at the time and I was five. In the fall a poisonous snake bit her and everybody wondered if she would die. I always liked to hear her tell about when it happened.

"It was dark that night, and I felt something wrap around my ankle and bite me. I knew it had to be a snake. 'I'm bit!'" Lovina recounted the experience. "Dena, my sister, panicked, but I went into the house and calmly stated that a snake bit me.

"'No!' my dad shouted in disbelief.

"'Right here. See two little fang holes! Right here!'

"My dad looked closely. 'Sure enough' he said. He grabbed a flashlight and ran outside looking for the snake but couldn't find it. He dashed off to get The Elder while Mother stayed by my bedside. I was in real bad pain all up and down my leg, but I finally dozed off.

"I heard somebody say 'The Elder is here,' and I had to go out where he was. My leg hurt so badly I couldn't walk. I had to hop on one foot. During his entire visit The Elder just talked. Finally he said for me to go to the water bucket and get a drink of water. I went to the bucket, took a drink, and came back and sat down. Then I threw up before I went back to bed. The Elder left.

"My leg swelled so big I couldn't wear anything on it

for a few weeks. I really got sick. I had no appetite and lost about ten pounds. I didn't have any wheelchair. I didn't even have crutches. I just hopped on one foot till the soreness went away. It was a poisonous snakebite, but we stuck with The Elder's rule — no doctors or hospitals or use of medicine or anything.

"I remember one Sabbath meeting at our house and I was in bed," Lovina continued. "The Elder made a big issue about me and asked me to come out. I hopped out. The Elder told everyone, 'Here's a young lady that was bitten by a deadly poisonous snake and has survived.' I was kind of disappointed that he didn't lay his hands on me and make me well immediately. I guess it was a miracle, and I had a lot of faith.

"The Elder seemed like a good person, and he told us to follow God. He said there might be a time that tribulations might come, and if you want to stand on what's right, a mother might have to watch someone slaughter her child. Now this put a terrible fear in me. There were times I felt sad before the snakebite, depressed I guess. I would walk to The Elder's place alone, and I talked to him awhile. He encouraged me. I always left feeling better. There was something calming about The Elder."

Lovina survived but not without a big ordeal and side affects. This scared everybody and made us even more cautious of snakes. We did gain a bit more respect for the power of a snake. We tried hard to fulfill orders from The Elder and kill all the snakes we could so the devil would not be in our midst. That was one of his rules to kill without offense. He reasoned that all snakes represented the devil.

She kept one big secret from all of us. Lovina had attended a public school and learned how to write poetry before she entered the colony. We were not allowed to write poetry, but she managed to write a poem while living in Lael Valley and kept it hidden throughout her stay there.

The Elder cut Grandma off from talking to her sister, Lydia, Lovina's mom. These sisters were very close. My grandmother felt deeply hurt by this and couldn't understand why. The Elder decided they spent too much time visiting, and he had given her this admonition, "This will prevent any unnecessary talking, and it is much better to be silent. Remember silence is golden, and the quieter you are the better." I remember how much this hurt Grandma, and she came to see us more often. She lived for the day The Elder would lift the ban he had placed on her but it never happened.

One Sabbath meeting at Abraham Schrock's home The Elder was preaching one of his messages of hell fire and brimstone. I lay down on a small blanket at Mom's feet for a nap, eyes still wide open, one ear to the floor. The Elder's exploding voice and its thunderous power echoing from the walls and ceiling caused it to vibrate. I felt scared from the force. Then a blood-thickening, hysterical scream filled the room startling me to my feet as the shrill sound moved quickly outside and continued off into the distance. Terror quaked inside me.

It was my cousin Freda Schrock screaming. She heard The Elder say, "There are some people here that will wish they had never been born. Some of you are in serious trouble with God, and one in here won't make it into heaven." I guess she thought she was the one. Freda Schrock was never the same, but The Elder remained unmoved from his rules and strange doctrines.

How much can intelligent people take? How long will they stay blinded?

The next fall Dad and the same working group had left for two months to pick cotton in Mississippi. They were isolated on the cotton plantation and never saw much outside the group who camped in tents there in the cotton fields. My Dad returned early that fall because he had had a nervous breakdown. Nobody knew why, and he was never the same. No one ever learned what really happened in those cotton fields in the Mississippi Delta. My real world was changing — had been changed forever! But what does a child know or understand about reality?

"Mom, why is Dad standing on top of the big, high

woodpile so long with an armload of wood?" I asked.

"It's getting cold, and he went out there to get firewood for the stove. I'll go out and see if he'll bring the wood in," Mom said as she grabbed a jacket. Returning with some wood for the stove Mom confided, "He's talking to himself, and I can't coax him into coming down and getting in here where it's warmer. It seems like that armload of wood would be too heavy to hold that long. I guess he has strong arms."

Dad continued this practice whenever he went outside for firewood. He would pick up an armload, climb to the top of the pile, and stand on top of it for hours, holding the wood and staring down at the woodpile talking to himself. He also wrote things in a tablet stating he feared some invisible powers were out to get him or kill him.

The Elder had recently made a new rule that nobody was allowed to go talk to him. Mom was desperate. She walked halfway to The Elder's place and called him. No answer. She walked closer and called again and then a third time. The Elder came and stood in the doorway. He listened as Mom pleaded for help and advice about what to do.

The Elder responded, "You are too carnal to understand spiritual things." And he closed the door.

Nobody knew what to do to help my dad. This was our new reality!

Patricia Hochstetler

Chapter 8

Questions

"Daddy, will you come to the creek bank with me and watch the minnows eat biscuit dough when I wash this mixing bowl?" I asked and waited

"Daddy, the minnows are hungry, will you come?" I begged and listened.

"Daddy, who are you talking to?" I asked and waited some more. *I'll just wait some more. Maybe he'll come.* "Daddy, why won't you talk to me?" A long quiet pause! Daddy looked traumatized.

"Daddy, why do you just stand there looking down? Why?" I begged for an answer. "Daddy, can you hear me? Oh, I'm sorry Dad. The Elder said that I'm not to call you Daddy. I forgot I'm to always call you Dad, and I will from now on. Why can't I call you Daddy? Will you please answer me if I call you Dad?" I waited and waited, but the roar of silence was deafening. *Well, my Daddy is gone. Is my Dad gone too? Why? My mommy is gone too. But I can say Mom and she answers me. When I forget and say Daddy or Mommy, am I in the red?*

"The minnows are hungry and I'll feed them before all the biscuit dough dries on the sides of the mixing bowl. Okay Dad?" I squatted down in front of him and looked up into his glassy eyes. Dad looked as if he never saw or noticed me at all, and I walked to the creek bank alone.

Silent conversations! *Minnows, here's your breakfast. I can see you are really hungry by the way you eat so fast. I wish you could talk to me. My dad can talk but he won't talk to me. He's talking now way up there in the yard. Why do you think he does that? I wish you could answer me. I know you would talk if you could. I better go or Mom will wonder where I am.*

I walked back toward our house. "Dad, I fed the minnows, and I'm going inside to help Mom with the dishes. Will you come inside too?" I pleaded. *Who is he talking to? Why won't he answer me?* My questions went unasked and unanswered.

"God, is my dad okay? He acts different. What's wrong with him? Will Dad be okay someday? God, I know you hear me, but why don't you talk to me? I wish I knew why. The Elder says you talk to him. Will you tell The Elder what will make my dad okay because he acts like something is terribly wrong? What is it? What will help Dad be like he was before? Will you please tell The Elder? Why does The Elder say we are too carnal to understand spiritual things? What are spiritual things? What are carnal things? What do those words mean? God, will you help my dad and my family? God, do you really test peoples' faith by things like this? Are you testing me by my dad not answering me?

"God, The Elder says You do test people like this. What should I do when my dad tells me to do something wrong, or when Dad accuses me of doing and saying things that I don't? You say in Ephesians 6:1, Children, obey your parents, and You say things to do and not do in Your Bible book. But what happens when it is impossible for me to do both? What if my dad expects me to say and do things that are wrong? What if my dad tells me to lie because he thinks something is a certain way and I know it isn't. Do I obey my dad like you say to do in Ephesians 6 and lie unlike what You say to do in the Bible? Or do I disobey my dad and always tell the truth? Why do I have to make this kind of decision? If I disobey Dad, I will be punished by him and maybe by You. If I obey Dad and disobey what You say in the Bible, will You punish me? Will I be in the red? Well, I'll do my best and hope you understand. And God, why is Mom so stressed? She's a mess. Please help Mom, too."

"Lois, come!" Mom called from the house. "We are going to see Grandma this morning."

"Is Daddy . . . I mean Dad going with us?" I asked.

"I can't coax him into coming along. I tried earlier," Mom answered. "Let's go. Your dad will stay here. He'll stand there talking till we come back."

We walked down the logging road to Grandma's. "Mom, why can't I say Mommy and Daddy any more?"

"Because The Elder said it's too worldish. We are to use Father and Mother or Dad and Mom."

"But why?"

"Because The Elder ordered it that way," Mom answered sternly.

"Why are Mom and Dad different than Mommy and Daddy?" I questioned.

"Rules are rules, and we are not to question them," Mom snapped.

I always liked going to see Grandma. Her three youngest children, my siblings, and I fed her goats leaves as she and Mom visited. But sometimes I stayed close and listened.

"Clarence is in bad shape. He stands and talks to himself most of the time," Mom said. "I don't know what to do about it. Sometimes he won't even eat with us."

"What causes it?" Grandma asked.

"I don't know. I went to The Elder for help, and he couldn't give me any advice. He only said that I was too carnal to understand spiritual things. That was all he had to say to me."

"I wonder why?" Grandma remarked. "It seems God would tell The Elder what to do to help Clarence and Luke. Luke's leg is in serious shape too. His leg is cut to the bone and infection has set in. Why can't this man of God lay hands on Clarence and Luke and heal them? Luke is only 14, just a child who miss cued with an axe while cutting wood. Luke's parents went to The Elder for advice. He blames Luke and it seems like Luke is to be a bad child now because he won't heal. The Elder repeatedly says, 'Luke must have bad thoughts or his leg would heal, and God punishes in different ways.'

"The Elder says to fast as atonement for sins in the colony

and many are fasting. I'm afraid too much. There's also something wrong with Susanna, Luke's sister. Her emotions seem to be getting her down and Christian and Lizzie (Susanna's parents) don't know why. The Elder judged Susanna to be the best of the four little girls that he had picked from four families. Now we don't know what is happening with Susanna. As for the other three, our Polly also seems depressed at times. Barbara has felt bad about the situation even though The Elder called her the good child. I don't know how Becky is reacting to The Elder's judgment." Grandma ended with a big sigh.

If Luke is bad because his leg won't heal, am I bad because I have toothaches so often? Is God punishing me? Do I need to fast more than on the Day of Atonement? I get so sick I don't know if I can fast like Mom and Dad and Grandma and Grandpa and many others. I don't know how they can fast two or three days. That might kill me. Maybe God thinks I have done some good because He healed my smashed thumb and the nail grew back. I wish He would stop my toothaches. I will try to be good and see if He will heal my teeth. Quaudy's tailbone injury slowly got better. Lovina lived after her snakebite. Fred survived his fall from a tree. I hope that Luke can be good enough for God to heal his leg. I have hope that God will heal my teeth. My thoughts and questions seemed endless.

Luke's dad, Christian, also hoped that Luke would be good and that God would chose to heal Luke's leg according to Grandma.

"'*Drech de auwa soo* (Press the eyes shut) *ova dreh die auwa von eppis es net recht goocha* (or turn your eyes if something doesn't look right,) keep going on and don't question anything The Elder says. It's gospel.' And those words are from my own brother, Christian Amstutz. So I guess we better stay humble and have faith like we are trained and accept whatever God allows," Grandma said, followed by a big sigh before continuing. "Another thing that I don't understand is why The Elder just changed his rules about the girls being partners. Now the girls are all free to come and go anywhere alone. I'm concerned since I felt they were all safer when they had a partner with them at all times even though it was very inconvenient and uncomfortable for them. The Elder has ordered that a girl's dormitory be built for our four oldest girls. Maybe Clarence can help build the girls' dormitory. He likes carpenter work, but is he able to do that now?"

"I don't know," Mom mumbled. "I better get back home and check on him."

When we arrived home, Dad still stood outside talking to himself or whomever he talked to.

The next week, the group that Dad had gone with to pick cotton in the Delta arrived back home in the valley. The colony was assembled together again for the Sabbath meeting. "We keep the laws according to God's orders and not like any worldly Jews or Amish. I want that understood. We go by the Bible, and you should know that by now," The Elder announced. "And blessed are the pure in heart."

It was not long until The Elder gave unusual instructions to Christian Amstutz.

"Christian, you know God told Abraham in the Bible to offer up his only son, Isaac, to show his faith. Abraham did, and God provided a way for him. Now I say to you, Christian, haul Joseph your eldest son out of the valley far away, so he cannot come back. Take him to the east coast and leave him. God will provide if you have faith. This meeting is dismissed."

Once home from the meeting in obedience to The Elder, Christian said to his wife, "You know some things don't look right, but if the man of God says it, you press your eyes shut and go on."

The next week on wash day, Grandma and Grandpa came walking slowly to our home. I ran to meet them. Grandpa said he was glad to be home after picking cotton. I was delighted to see him, but he was very thin and carried a heavy look. I walked with them but they were quiet. Dust puffed up each time Grandma's bare feet hit the dusty road. Once in our yard, I listened as they talked to Mom.

"You know The Elder ordered Christian to haul Joseph to the east coast twenty-four hours after that last meeting and leave him there," Grandpa moaned.

"*Achduleeva! Fa vos?* (Unbelievable! What for?)" Mom shouted.

"Words Joseph said about the Passover being in the spring and not in the fall must have gotten back to The Elder," Grandpa said.

"Why Joseph? He's my nephew and this can't happen to him. He's only 20-years-old and a nice boy. He's not been in the world much and doesn't know how to live in it any more than a ten-year-old child would. The Amish relatives in Delaware won't accept him because of the *mieding* (shunning) on our families," Grandma whimpered.

"The Elder said to give him one hundred dollars and dump him in Delaware," Grandpa said. "They had the money since we worked picking cotton. Age twenty is what The Elder has declared our legal age for adulthood now. It's not eighteen or twenty-one like the world people say."

"Christian held on to his words, 'Press the eyes shut or turn your eyes if something doesn't look right, keep going on and don't question anything that The Elder says. It's gospel.' I don't know how Christian can stand this," Grandma said. "Lizzie is flying apart over her oldest son being ordered dumped. She fears for his survival and what will happen to him. Joseph doesn't know it yet. They will tell him tomorrow after he's in the truck going that he will not come back and is going to the east coast to live."

As scheduled, after that pronouncement Christian Amstutz drove his son, Joseph, to Delaware, gave him one hundred dollars, and left him near some Amish relatives Joseph did not know. Joseph was on his own, deserted by his father who put him out of his truck and then turned around and went back to the colony. Will we ever hear if Joseph survived? What happened to him remains a mystery.

During another visit Grandpa asked, "Is Clarence any better than when he left the cotton plantation early?"

"No! He seems worse."

"If The Elder orders Clarence hauled off, I don't want you and the grandchildren to go," Grandpa said. "If you have to, eat soap, and be *kronk on cuts* (sick and vomit) so you won't be forced to leave."

Grandma and Grandpa Miller left disturbed.

"Mom, why did Joseph get hauled away?" I asked.

"Because he disobeyed."

"Is he bad like Luke?"

"To disobey is bad."

"Will The Elder make them haul Luke off and dump him too?"

"I don't know, and I don't want to talk about it," Mom snapped. "Let's go milk the goats."

"Okay!" I walked quietly alongside Mom to the barn.

Why did this have to happen to Joseph? I thought Joseph was 17 and just one of the big children in our colony. Will this happen to me if I disobey? Will I ever be hauled off and dumped on the east coast wherever that is? It sounds like a long way away from us, so Joseph will never find his way back. That scares me. Was God really testing Christian and Lizzie's faith like Abraham in the Bible? I had more troubled thoughts.

What happened to The Elder? Why did he begin preaching louder sermons patterned from some books that he had ordered, but he wouldn't allow those books in our school? Why didn't he continue lecturing only from the King James Bible? He formed some of his sermons after The Little Red Hen, The Fox and the Crows, and Aladdin's Lamp. Some felt the boy in The Elder's story was directed at Rudy Schrock. Ali Baba and the Forty Thieves was another story he used to model a sermon.

He had one sermon he repeatedly gave about the seven virgins; it was taken from the Bible. He formed his own messages and would indirectly direct them at somebody in the colony. For example, he used The Seven Virgins story referring to my mom's seven sisters as the seven virgins. We knew without him saying it.

He also had a sermon about Lot's wife who turned to a pillar of salt. He gave a message designed about the thieves on the cross beside Jesus. His messages were often about folks who lived in the mountains. They were more like fairy tales according to some colony members. He also preached from the Bible using a parable style leaving some wondering what he really said or meant. Why?

I wasn't the only one asking questions. In hushed tones you might hear questions voiced confidentially. No one dared identify the questioner. Why did he preach that somebody in the colony was not going to make it into heaven and would go to hell? That's the meeting that my cousin Freda Schrock got up and ran out screaming. Freda believed it was her that The Elder was talking about. That incident frightened me. Why is Freda not normal yet? Why won't she eat or talk much? What will happen to her? Is she bad too? Why can't The Elder help Freda feel better? Is she really going to hell?

Grandma's eyes were red so much of the time, and she doesn't have allergies. Surely she can't be crying a lot, can she? I know she desperately wants The Elder to lift the *bann* (ban) he placed on her visiting with her sister, and she wants to get in the good graces with God. Why can't she? Grandma is too nice to hurt like this. Freda is Grandma's niece, her sister Lydia's daughter, and Grandma wants to see Lydia and talk to her. Lizzie Amstutz spoke to Lydia, and Lydia said how much she wanted to visit with Grandma. I wonder *is Grandma in the red now for wanting all this? Why is Grandma getting so quiet?*

I thought about Grandpa and the time he cut my sister's hair when she caught it in barbed wire. I remembered wanting sweetness and eating sugar. I listened to people talk about fasting and wondered *should I fast for wanting sweet things?* Lots of people are fasting. *Can everybody be in the red,* I wondered. *What for?*

The Elder ordered the colony to build a girl's dormitory for my mom's seven sisters — God's chosen seven virgins as he called them. Why?

"The girls house will be built L-shaped, three rooms one way and two the other," The Elder ordered. "Make special hiding places in the walls to store jars of canned food to reserve for hard times that are coming. Dig a hideout shelter for safety from the enemy; make an underground tunnel to it with a hidden secret door. This is for protection," he said.

I don't know if he felt scared of bombs, evil spirits, or people. He wanted to feel safely protected from whatever he feared. He expected horrible things to happen. He called it hard times. The Elder believed it's important to have hidden food and shelter.

"When tribulation comes, follow God," The Elder commanded. "Stand on what's right. If you're told you will be killed if you believe in God or have a Bible and you're asked if you believe in God or have a Bible, say yes! Be prepared to die for your faith. You mother's might have to watch somebody kill your children."

Dad helped build the dormitory in the woods south of our home and west of Grandpa's. It was to be built in stages. The first three rooms were built, and Mom's four oldest sisters stayed in two rooms, two girls to a room. The Elder stayed in the third room. The concrete foundation for the last two rooms was poured, but those two rooms were never finished. The four girls staying in the dormitory helped relieve Grandpa's small house of overcrowding. Daily The Elder and the four girls walked to Grandma and Grandpa's house for all three meals.

Later The Elder ordered them to build him a separate room on the west-end of the girl's dormitory putting some distances between his living quarters and my aunts. A ten-foot boardwalk led from the dormitory to his room. He spoke of being a eunuch and said how vexed he felt, but he did have some favorite people in the colony.

The Elder had a print shop set up in the girls' dormitory. He spent time writing and planning books which he had my aunts type and print for him. Aunt Ruby served as his typist. Naomi, Erma, and Martha San followed his orders printing, cutting papers, and binding books. They made a lot of scripture line books and The Elder's El-Elohe-Israel books.

One evening while walking back to the girls' dormitory after supper at Grandma's, Aunt Martha San found the largest rattlesnake anybody had ever found in this valley, and she killed it.

After The Elder heard the story he declared, "That's the way to get rid of the evil in this valley. Those snakes represent the Devil. Kill'em all!"

One day in school The Elder, displeased by something he thought he saw or heard, ordered Delilah Miller, our teacher, to meet with him after school in his room on the back of the schoolhouse. Something was wrong!

Questions were multiplying! Suspicion was raising its ugly head? What was happening in the middle of this timberland jungle and on our promised land?

What about The Elder? What about The Elder's rules? What about The Elder's indoctrination? What about the members of the colony? What about the secrecy?

Time is not only the great healer. Time is also the great revealer! The questions will be answered!

Chapter 9

Teacher Ousted & Schoolbooks Burned

People were not prepared for the rage and flaming torch of anger that swept through our once peaceful, promised land and colony. Irritation erupted into action, and every word and every move focused on those The Elder perceived to be erring colony members.

The first person cut off from the colony was my great aunt, our schoolteacher, Delilah Miller. Barely five feet tall, very petite, round-faced, brown-eyed, brunette, super energetic, and courageous, she was an enthusiastic and witty lady in her early thirties.

When she moved into the valley, Delilah lived in her 8x12 house trailer she bought in Mississippi. Before long the colony switched her into Abraham Schrock's newly built 8x16 chicken house and gave The Elder her trailer. He had the best living conditions until on his orders a room was built onto the back of the schoolhouse solely for him.

"The Elder prophet is a special man of God, and I'm honored to give up my trailer for him to live in," Aunt Delilah said. "I'm very satisfied and comfortable living in the new chicken house. I utilized the two nice little 8x8 rooms. My bed is in one room, and the kitchen is in the other. I nailed a seat board to the kitchen wall by my table. I put plain colored linoleum on the floor and on a twelve-inch board counter top that I made. I fixed it up. I feel up town, and it's modern for us. I'm the only one living here in the valley with linoleum. My goat and chickens stay together in that little shack in my side yard. I'm happy."

Delilah had taught two years in the Amish church school

in Aberdeen, Mississippi. This Amish group had moved from Pensacola, Florida, because the public school situation there was strict. They moved soon after they found out Mississippi did not enforce the school laws. Mississippi State school officials gave them permission for their own school and furnished the books. The Amish insisted on having their own teacher, and the state gave Delilah a teaching certificate. This happened before The Elder arrived in Aberdeen and led his group away from the Amish.

Delilah also taught about four years in Hamilton, Mississippi, under The Elder's scrutiny. After moving to Tennessee, she taught about two years in Lael Parochial School. Having taught many of her pupils for eight years, she was well liked and admired by the students. Her students had always called her *Daly*, her Pennsylvania Dutch name. The Elder called her Delilah until our first year in the Tennessee oak valley when he announced. "Delilah was a conniving, sneaky woman in the Bible. Our schoolteacher shouldn't be carrying a name with that kind of connotation. Now I order everyone to call her Dee. No more *Daly* or Delilah."

After two satisfactory years of teaching at Lael Parochial School in Tennessee, The Elder confronted Dee. "Why do you have flowers in the wooded yard around your chicken house and goat shed? You know planting flowers is against the rules."

"I never planted the wild flowers there. God did! Would God want me to destroy what he allowed?" Dee asked eagerly.

I don't know if Dee cut the flowers down or not, but that was not their last encounter. Later she and The Elder had a lively discussion — and disagreement — about the way eggs from grocery stores were placed in egg cartons. Dee requested a box of eggs the next time Christian went to town. She showed The Elder how eggs were supposed to be placed in the carton, and he was wrong. This did not go over well with The Elder.

Shortly after the egg incident The Elder wrote Dee a

note accusing her of talking bad to the school children. She ignored the note knowing she had not said anything bad, and she feared to respond.

One day soon after receiving the note The Elder approached her in an accusing spirit. "Dee, you will meet with me in my room after school today."

"What in the word of wisdom could this be for?" the students asked. That afternoon as the children walked home from school, Dee went into The Elder's efficiency room attached to the back of the schoolhouse. He was expecting her and his bearing indicated it was not going to be pleasant.

With a thrust forward in his step and a threat in his voice The Elder asked, "Dee, what are the first words you say to the school children right after you excuse them for recess?"

"I tell them to go to the toilet and get water."

"That's not what I hear you say," The Elder retorted.

"What do you think I say then?"

"You say, 'Children, go to the toilet and make water.' That's *not* the way to talk to children," The Elder chided.

"You must have misunderstood me. I don't say 'make water.' I say 'get water.'" Dee responded defensively.

The Elder shouted, "Almighty God knows what you say, and I heard you too! We will take care of this matter later. You are excused."

Later Aunt Dee came to talk to my mom.

"I thoroughly enjoy teaching and the children, Mary. I feel I'm accomplishing something good and worthwhile helping the children learn and being a part of the colony. I feel like I'm contributing to the group and making the wheels turn in every family. That's important and it feels good," Aunt Dee humbly confided. "I got geography books, but The Elder didn't want me to have them. I wanted the children to learn about the world we live in. I wanted them to learn more than just the ABC's, writing, and arithmetic. That's all The Elder wanted — just reading, writing, and arithmetic. I guess that is the basics of learning. I also had a problem with The Elder about allowing me to get dictionaries so all the

111

students had access to one. I thought that was straightened out. I wonder if he is still upset over that."

"Aunt Dee, I'll never forget you teaching me to trace, cut out, and paste," I interrupted. "I traced on paper around your little boat pattern and cut it out. Then Aunt Kay helped me glue the boats three corners together. That was fun. We let it dry till the next day. Then you told a bunch of us we could put our little boats in the creek there beside the schoolhouse at recess. You said if we made our boats well, they would float away down the stream and out of sight. And you said if we made them poorly they would get water in them and sink to the creek bottom and wash away. We all put our boats in the water and watched them float away. I can still see my little boat going to the side, drifting a long way down that gentle creek, and floating out of sight. I learned a lot and enjoyed watching my boat float away. I saw some boats sink."

"I'm glad you enjoyed the boats because that will be the last time we do it. The Elder says it's too much like playing. I didn't view it as playing. I liked to do all kinds of little things like that to bring some joy to the children," Aunt Dee added. "I thought it was educational and not bad. We didn't have a lot of expense in it. I liked the times we got free cigar boxes and covered all the *schmucha* (ornamental) stuff with wallpaper, material scraps, or whatever it took. We put partitions in some of them. We made all kinds of things with those boxes, didn't we? They're your cherished little pencil boxes."

"Aunt Dee, I like you. You're my first and best schoolteacher. I'll get my precious little box now so you can see I still have it." I dashed to my room.

"Mary, Lois is an excellent student with A+ grades. Have you noticed she has a very distinctly, strange walk? One foot goes over the other when she walks. I'll always remember her as the little girl that was pigeon toed. Did you know that?"

"Yes, she's pigeon toed, and sometimes she falls over her own feet and lands flat on her face. I don't know why,"

112

Mom shared.

"Lois is my youngest student, but she learns fast. She was only four when we put her in first grade with her brother, Fred, and he was five. She's done great. I enjoy watching them walk from the last bend on that dirt road coming to school, and I know you're around the other bend watching." She paused before adding, "Lois was Patricia before The Elder changed her name, wasn't she?"

"Here's my precious little box. I like it so much. See what all I keep in it? Here's a tiny pencil, little erasers, and. . . ."

"Lois, I'm glad you like your box so much."

Then she turned to Mom, "Mary, it's such a joy to see Lois learn and grow like she is. I have to tell you that coming here I met my brother, Benjamin, your father, on the timber road and what he said shocked me. He said 'Whatever The Elder says is true whether we know it or not. You don't question anything. Nothing! It doesn't make any difference. If The Elder said you killed a man, you killed a man.' That scares me."

"That would be scary," Mom replied.

Soon without Dee knowing it The Elder called a meeting with the fathers of each family. A decision was made to ask each child individually what words their teacher says immediately after excusing them for recess. The answers came back. Each child said the same as the teacher, 'Go to the toilet and get water.' This proved nothing to The Elder who declared, "The children didn't hear Dee right. I know what I heard through the wall, and God doesn't lie." No one asked what God had to do with his hearing.

After that the issue was not what Dee said to the children. Now she was accused of calling The Elder a liar and putting him down by calmly claiming he misunderstood her. Why did she question him? Everybody knew you did not dispute anything The Elder said.

"Dee, you are now cut off from teaching and from everyone in the colony." The Elder announced.

The Elder called another meeting for all the fathers. "Fathers, get everything your children ever got from Dee or

113

the school and return it to her or burn it immediately," he ordered.

Susanna Amstutz, a 12-year-old Lael student, shared her feelings, "I didn't like it when my father collected everything we had ever gotten from Dee. It didn't matter if it was a half used up eraser, the stub of a pencil, a rubber band, a piece of paper, or anything that came through the school or Dee. We had to give everything like that to Father to burn. I had a tiny chest made of my only two matchboxes. They were glued together one on top of the other and then covered with wallpaper except the end where we sewed buttons so we could pull out the two drawers. Dee helped me make it in school. This little matchbox chest was very special to me. In it I kept the half pencils allotted me, the erasers, rubber bands, buttons, and any treasure I had. I felt so sad, but I still was forced to give up my precious little matchbox treasure chest. I don't know what actually happened to it."

The fathers, obedient to The Elder, took all the children's prized accumulation and returned it to Dee. "We do not want this contaminated stuff!" Shortly after this incident The Elder separated the school children. The boys were to be on one side of the classroom and schoolyard, and the girls were put on the other side.

The Elder issued another order. "Abraham Schrock, haul the heifer (Dee Miller) out of the valley immediately. I have excommunicated her. She is like Jezebel in the Bible — a wicked woman and a skunk. She's removed from our members now, and we will carry on with our school without her."

At The Elder's appointed time, Abraham hauled Dee out of the valley and left her at a bus station. The Elder announced, "Your evil teacher, the skunk, is gone now and we will continue with Lael Parochial School. First we must have a schoolbook burning ceremony and burn all those contaminated books that this corrupt woman taught from. I must clean house. Everything will go that she had anything to do with. I appoint Naomi Miller as the new schoolteacher."

Frank Schrock was older than I, so he had to help destroy all the evidence. I was too young to understand what was happening, and he tried to explain it to me.

"I remember The Elder went into a rage about Dee, our teacher, and excommunicated her. He ordered our good schoolbooks, even the Row Peterson ones, to be burned. I had to carry load after load of books from the schoolhouse, across the creek bridge, and to the sawmill near my house. The Elder made us rip all the pages out of each book and put them in the fire to make sure they burned. I even had to throw the book spine in the fire too." I had no idea what a book spine was, but Frank went right on talking.

"I liked my teacher and the books. My favorite book was *If I Were Zody.* This book was about a young fellow who went to Europe and about how people in Holland wore wooden shoes. History was my favorite subject. We were beginning to study geography, and it was interesting to hear what was going on in other parts of the world. I had to help carry all those favorite books to the bonfire. I don't know why but The Elder was impressed with how eager Rudy, my brother, was helping with tearing up the books." That was his explanation. When he finished, he walked away.

Most of the children were obviously distraught over losing their well-liked and admired teacher and their books. Something more had to be done to erase her influence and memory. The Elder roared, "Now go set fire to the skunk's buildings and burn them to help rid us of the evidence of that wicked woman, Delilah!"

Flames resembling hell fire The Elder had spoken of often now engulfed the little chicken house that Aunt Dee had been living in and her goat shed that was close by. Surprisingly somebody outside Lael Valley became concerned about a forest fire and called the fire department. Christian Amstutz had a hard task explaining and convincing the fireman that the fire was set on purpose to destroy a couple of buildings and that it really was controlled and okay.

I was convinced my first teacher was evil and would burn in hell on judgment day. By the end of the day two large piles of ashes were the only signs in the valley that Dee had been our teacher. Then The Elder ordered the colony to fast and pray for two days over the situation. Frank and some of the rest of us got sick while fasting on The Day of Atonement once a year, but this fasting was twice as bad."

They bought some new books, but it wasn't the same. Many books were never replaced. This issue was quite an ordeal for me. Now there were more questions, more frustrations, and more anger. What *was* happening in the middle of this timberland jungle and on our promised land? What could anybody do?

Chapter 10

Excommunication

Several people in Lael Valley were beginning to come under the sharp double-edged axe and were deeply cut in different ways. Their lives were either cut off from the colony or cut into diverse angles emotionally. It slashed hearts, minds, and spirits. Lives and families were torn apart. For some, our paradise valley became a death valley. Hope was waning. Regardless of who was involved and what action was taken, it was always The Elder who made the decisions.

The Elder called another meeting and proclaimed, "Willie Miller and Mattie Miller must also be cut off from the colony. They must leave like their wicked sister, Delilah. Abraham Schrock, you are my right hand man. You tell them, and then haul them out of the village, out of this valley, and completely off this land."

"What have they done?" Abraham asked. "Willie is my right hand man at the sawmill. I need him there! What did he do?"

"When God says they must go, they must go! That's all there is to it, so act now," The Elder retorted.

Abraham insisting inquired again. "Can you give us one reason for their excommunication?"

"They are like minded as their sister Delilah, the skunk, and they must go. There will be no time for confessions or questions. Now obey God's command, Abraham."

It was a sad day when Abraham set a time to haul Willie and Mattie out of the valley. Willie went willingly, but Mattie resisted, "I have no place to go. Mother's and Father's church excommunicated me because I followed The Elder whom I still believe in. Neither my parents nor anyone from their Amish church will accept me because of their *mieding* (shunning). I don't know where sister Dee is by now, and I don't know of any place to go. I'm not going!"

Mattie, unwelcome in the village or to work at the sawmill or do anything with the colony anymore, walked the woods daily with her dog, Coy. Nobody would talk to her or acknowledge her in any way. During the meeting one Sabbath Coy came to the door. Everyone knew Mattie roamed in the near-by woods hiding with channeled ears trying to catch a word of worship and what was going on. "Why doesn't she give up and leave as God commands?" some members asked with great regularity.

Weeks later, darkness shadowed the valley one evening and hungry, bony Coy got into somebody's chickens creating quite a ruckus. Then crunch, crunch, crunch, deep into the wood flickered a flashlight. Mattie was prowling around the houses again hoping to hear a familiar voice or get a glimpse of some family member. Hungry and lonely she went to my grandpa's gate and pleaded for something to eat. After all Grandpa was her oldest brother. Grandpa asked The Elder, "What should I do?"

"Don't feed her. When she runs completely out of food and gets hungry enough, she will leave," The Elder responded.

Grandpa followed The Elder's advice. The colony knew Mattie was left to starve in the woods or leave the valley. Lizzie Amstutz, Mattie's sister, never asked The Elder about feeding Mattie's dog so he would not get into their chickens and kill them. After dark so nobody would see it or know about it, Lizzie put leftover food at their gate for Coy. She slipped some on top of the gatepost not knowing if her sister found it before the wild animals did.

Once again the attention turned to Luke, the 14-year-old son of Christian and Lizzie Amstutz. Luke's leg remained swollen and wouldn't heal. The Elder had forbidden members to seek advice from him but in a meeting he announced, "If Luke is good enough and has enough faith,

118

his leg will heal if it be God's will. Remember it's faith and God that heals, not doctors. Let God do his work."

They made Luke crutches from small green trees and left him to heal naturally. He learned to use his homemade crutches, but he was not able to work. Horrible infection invaded his leg all the way to the bone. His mom, Lizzie, wondered if she was in the red and if this was a curse on her family for putting food out supposedly for Mattie's dog, Coy, when it was really for Mattie. Lizzie became perplexed over her son's and sister's situations.

Nobody had heard a word from Joseph Amstutz. Everybody wondered what had happened to him once he was dumped on the east coast. He was never given the colony address and had no way of contacting any family. Christian continued to say, "You know some things don't look right, but if the man of God says it, you press your eyes shut and go on."

As a small child, I continually heard that my cousin Joseph was hauled off and dumped 'for being disobedient' as The Elder put it. This scared me. I feared that if I did anything wrong I would be dumped somewhere too without an explanation. What happened to Uncle Willie, and where is Aunt Dee, my teacher? Why did Aunt Mattie have to wander in the woods so long starving until she walked outside the oak walls of our commune and sold bony Coy, her dog, and only friend, to buy a bus ticket? I heard she found somebody to take her to the bus station and bought a ticket to Akron, Ohio. *Did she ever get to Akron? What happened to her?* I wondered.

I remember going with my mom to the Schrock's home to visit. Six year old Joe Schrock, black hair, brown eyes, and very shy, sat on the ground on the sunny south side of their house. As we got closer, I could see he had little roads made in the dirt and had some dirt piled up for hills. He had stones for his horses and wagons, trucks, and tractors, and was making his stone vehicles go around on his tiny roads. He was playing! When we returned home, I had plenty of questions stored up.

"Mom, Joe was playing."

"Oh, I don't think so."

"Yes he was. I could tell. Why did he get to play, but you won't let me? You said nobody was supposed to play."

She reaffirmed that nobody was to play. "Well, maybe he was not doing what he was supposed to do."

"Nobody made him stop. They just let him play. Why?"

"Lois, just because someone else did something wrong has little to do with you."

"It's not fair!"

"That's true, but you should not do wrong because someone else does. Two wrongs don't make any right." Mom explained.

"Two wrongs don't make any right," I repeated. I was easily convinced.

Before we left the Schrock's, Joe had whispered to me, "I'm scared when The Elder preaches. I heard him say that some people will wish they were never born, and I cried. Remember when the bridge to the schoolhouse washed out when we had that storm. I really liked that." I didn't tell him that I didn't like it.

I wondered why his parents allowed him to play. Something else bothered me too. Why didn't Joe's parents not call his younger brother Gad like The Elder had instructed? Some of them called him Howard, his birth name. Why? It was obvious Abraham was becoming more lenient with his children.

Trouble was brewing. It was not long until The Elder announced, "Abraham is in the red (bad) and has done something wrong, and we will get to the bottom of this problem."

Fear of the unknown cut as an axe into the colony members' minds. What would happen next?

I hurt for my Grandma Miller because we could go see Joe's mom, her sister, and Aunt Lydia, but she couldn't. Grandma still couldn't talk to Lydia because The Elder's orders had cut her off from talking to her, and he would not lift the ban.

That's not the only strange thing going on. He had all the married couples split apart, and he taught celibacy – whatever that meant.

The Elder became more and more upset with Abraham, his right hand man. Disagreements over financial issues at the sawmill broke out. The Elder accused Abraham of keeping more than his share of money from timber sales. More logs seemed to be going out, and all the families received no more money than before. The Elder began calling Abraham the bull of Bashan like in the Bible. I didn't understand why.

The meetings seemed heated now, and I was scared when The Elder shouted and his thunder rolled. I didn't really know why he yelled so much. He was supposed to be a holy man that God talked to. I knew things were not okay. It was going to get worse.

In just a few days The Elder issued another edict. "Every family will be on its own and separated for now. Don't talk to others outside your own family."

Our visits with the Schrocks ended immediately.

Even as young as I was, I knew tension was building. Finally one day The Elder went to where some fathers were working. As he approached, Abraham didn't take off his hat as The Elder had trained the men to do whenever he came around. It was in reverence to him, the man of God.

"Why you look terrible with that hat on your head," The Elder remarked to Abraham.

Abraham listened without a move and replied, "It seems man's commandments are growing around here like wild weeds."

"God will deal with the wicked and unjust," The Elder answered back. "There will be a meeting with the fathers at the schoolhouse tomorrow at seven o'clock in the evening."

The fathers including Abraham went to the meeting. The Elder didn't lecture long before he announced, "Abraham, you are now excommunicated from the colony. Your entire family is excommunicated, all 17 of you. None of you can attend our meetings or Lael School. Lael valley

121

land, all 2,005 acres of it, will be divided among all the families."

Chapter 11

Chaos

What was happening with God's chosen people and our promised land that was to flow with milk and honey? Was it only a new tower of Babel? Was it a new trek through the wilderness for the Children of Israel? Confusion reigned! Food supplies diminished, and the land was proving to be too rocky for farming. No one could make a living on this land. The Elder split up families, and now he announced our promised land is to be divided.

Uncle Willie and Aunt Mattie were excommunicated as well as Aunt Dee, my teacher. The Elder referred to my teacher as Jezebel, a heifer, and a skunk. How stinky and bad that sounded to me! I knew I would never see any of them again and assumed they would go to hell with the wicked as The Elder had stated.

Luke's condition had worsened. *Why doesn't God want Luke's leg to heal,* I wondered? *What would God do to me if I had an accident and got hurt?*

This entire situation - the accident, the lack of medical attention, and no healing - began affecting him emotionally. Luke sat at the table with his head down during the entire meal as *rutz* (snot) dripped on his cold empty plate. He would not eat or look at anyone and finally refused to go to the table altogether. After a year – and by his choice – he started staying in a small shed separated like a leper from his family. Meals were taken to him. He sometimes ate a little, but often after the person who brought the meal had gone, he threw the food out. Finally it escalated to throwing the food and the plates and breaking them. He was scolded for his actions, so he vacated the shed before his meals arrived. Once the person delivering his meal left he returned to the shed, nibbled at the food, and threw the rest away. Eventually he stayed at the edge of nearby woods to avoid prying eyes.

The Elder ordered special fasting and prayers in the colony on Luke's behalf, but there was no human intervention to the situation caused by a lack of medical attention. This is our utopia? Was this all the man of God could do? What was the power The Elder possessed that kept intelligent human beings from helping a suffering child? He did this in the name of God!

Sixteen year old Mary Amstutz, Luke's oldest sister, became upset with all that had happened. She took a stand on a trivial issue, but at least she reacted to her environment. She challenged The Elder about wearing his heavy strap designed dresses and ankle length under pants. Mary addressed him, "If you can show me in the Bible where I should wear long heavy clothes like those, I will."

The Elder never showed her a scripture, and she refused to wear his designed clothes. He took action by issuing this order, "Use a severe *mieding* (shunning) on Mary in the family until she straightens up. Don't talk to her or give her any food at the table. Reach around her and pass the food bowls to the next person. Don't let her work or even help with anything."

Mary reacted. After the serving bowls of food were passed around her and placed in the middle of the table, in a spirit of defiance she got up, reached for the food, served herself, and ate what she wanted. She won the battle for food, and she continued to wear her shorter under pants and old Amish type long dresses. But The Elder extracted a price, additional heartbreak!

"The Elder told my family to shun me and cut me off from everything," I heard her crying. "I can't wash clothes, dishes, or floors, do any cooking, sewing, or milking. Nothing! I read the Bible a lot. My family talks to our dog, Shep, but not to me. I thought they would change, but they haven't. It's hard to live like this and I'm feeling numb. Things are

124

getting kind of vague in my mind, and I don't know why."

This is love? I silently questioned. I could not comprehend what was happening, but I knew what it meant to hurt, and this family . . . my relatives . . . were hurting. They were becoming a divided unit torn, shredded, and cut by bitter reality. But the end was not in sight.

Mary Amstutz took the freedom to speak to my mom, and I was listening. She repeated the story about Joseph being dumped. I guess she needed to relive the experience. "The Elder went into a rage and raised his voice and raved at my brother, Joseph. Father came home from the sawmill and told us The Elder had given word to haul him away. Father told Joseph to pack up his things. He did, and they left. Later father came back alone, and we don't know what happened to Joseph. My father won't talk about it. Now my mother's afraid The Elder will order me hauled off like Joseph. I'm scared, but sometimes I wish he would," Mary choked out.

"I'm afraid for you, too, but I'm afraid to talk," Mom answered. I don't know what to say to you about these situations. I'm afraid to say much of anything. And I don't know what will happen with Clarence's situation either, so I better be quiet."

Mary slowly walked toward her home with her head down low.

Utopia . . . reality? Even a young child reacts to tension. The unasked question, "Did we leave Elkhart for this?" must surely have gone through my mind. The God I knew in childish faith was surely unlike the heartless and demanding man that we called The Elder!

The Elder's sermons were taking strange directions. He continued giving sermons patterned after the books he had ordered. Some people felt sermons from these books were directed at Abraham Schrock. He had sermons about folks who lived in the mountains that were more like fairy tales, but some of his sermons still came from the Bible.

After one sermon The Elder looked at Susanna and said, "Those were not my words but the words of God."

Most of the people didn't know what he meant. Susanna

Amstutz sat silent. It seemed a mystery to Christian and Lizzie Amstutz as to why their daughter, Susanna, had sunk into such complacency and depression. At the age of ten she had been chosen by The Elder as the best of the little girls that he had picked from four families. At thirteen Susanna could not tell a soul her secret.

It's difficult to tell Susanna's story, but the depth of chaos would not be revealed without it. This is her story:

"The deep kept secret bounced around in my head daily. I heard him clearly say, 'Susanna, you are more than likely going to hell. And if you miss hell it'll be by a very narrow escape. These words are not my words. They are the words of God.' He nodded his head to reinforce his words.

"The Elder went on walking the other way. I didn't understand why he was standing at the creek bridge on Swanegan Branch Road, or why he stopped me as I was walking home alone after cleaning the schoolhouse? Why?

"I felt numb all over. My mind was a fiery blur. I knew I couldn't tell a soul on earth. I'm worried what will happen to me next. Father would believe anything The Elder said because as he often says, '*drech* (press) the eyes closed and keep going and don't question anything. It's gospel.' I feel doomed. I am doomed! I feel doomed to hell now.

"I prayed, God, show me now what I need to do so I won't go to hell. Please God, forgive my terrible sin that would send me to hell. This feels torturous. I'll fast four days from all food and water. Like David in the Psalms, I pray, 'Create in me a clean heart O God and renew a right spirit within me.' I feel the desperation of Job. I long for the times when I feel innocent and don't know the awful burden of this doom. God, why would You condemn me? A verse in the Bible says, 'God made everything for himself, even the wicked for the day of evil'

"I think You must have made me for the day of evil. I don't feel I have a chance. Neither was I given any choice. God, it doesn't seem like You are loving, kind, or fair to me. This is extremely difficult for me. Nobody knows what The Elder told me except You and me. Maybe that's to my advantage. That way there are no reminders of it except the ones from You through The Elder and those I give myself. But what have I done wrong? Is it because I didn't want to do a chore, or I wanted something a different color? Or did I think something bad and didn't know it?

"Once more I heard The Elder's voice saying 'Susanna, you are more than likely going to hell. And if you miss hell it'll be by a very narrow escape. These words are not my words; they're the words of God.' That's what The Elder said. Why do his words tumble in my head over and over?

"God, I can't sleep tonight. I can only sin by crying. I'm weak and unworthy. Please don't let me wake up to see another day. Yesterday, as I hung clothes on the line, I wanted to make them look good. I shook them, straightened the belts, pulled wrinkles out of them, and my father looked at me with those eyes of disapproval and said, 'Favor is deceitful and beauty is vain but a woman that fears the Lord she shall be praised.' I've been told this over and over by The Elder and my father.

"I feel like I've been cut down to the ground again and again just because I tried to make our clothes look neat or try to do what's good. I'm open game and a target at any given time just like my brothers, Joseph and Luke, and now my sister, Mary, too. I feel no secure feelings and no safe place. I have no protection. When The Elder says, 'God told me' I can't say or do anything that might defy that. So there's no comfort even in You, God, because I can't trust You either."

That was Susanna's story.

Who knows what it means? We could only see and feel the heartbreak.

I was struggling with my own world. What will happen to my dad? Is he really bad? He's upset, and nobody can help him. Why? God knows, and I hope He will help. Is Dad's condition a living parable that will be over someday? In the increasing stress in our troubled colony no one had time to answer my questions.

The list of problems had only begun. Additions to that list seemed unending. For instance: What will happen to my cousin Freda Schrock now? Since she ran out of that one meeting screaming, she's afraid she will be one of those people The Elder spoke of who won't make it into heaven and will wish they were never born.

Why does she sit and rock back and forth for months and often won't eat much or talk? Why did The Elder excommunicate the entire Abraham Schrock family? Was it because of Joe's playing or Freda's screaming? What else could it be? Is disobedience what happened again?

The Elder repeatedly said, "Nobody is allowed to freely come visit me if they have a question. Now all of you know the rules after ten years. Observe them if I'm not here. I won't die a natural death for I am a man of God. If I'm killed for my faith or caught up in a cloud and disappear like Elijah, abide by the rules which God has given. Keep the rules and laws faithfully on your own and God will bless you. I must warn you to prepare for hard times and great tribulations for God's people as the Bible tells us. I say again prepare for those tribulations and hard times. Read the Bible and that book I ordered, *The Pilgrim's Progress* by John Bunyan. Strive to be God's pilgrims for the rest of your life."

Then there was the Elder's shocking announcement. "Each family will be on its own." We, like all the other members of the colony, had come from various parts of the country to be one family, God's family.

"Don't depend on each other," was an even more devastating pronouncement. Our lives were intertwined. We were family. What was the Elder doing? Were these the seeds of distrust or words of wisdom? What did he know that he was unwilling to tell us?

"You might be killed, separated, or scattered all over the earth," he preached. "There are only a few other people in the world who believe like us . . . God's way . . . the only right way. Stick with the truth if you want to be in the 144,000 of God's chosen people. The Tennessee valley land will soon be split up between the families. Never sell your portion of land. It was God's land to start with. Let it go back to God. He gave the land to us, and He can take it away from us.

When this happens, don't look back like Lot's wife. She looked back and turned into a pillar of salt. Practice not looking back."

Looking backward when walking became an issue. We tried to look forward all the time. If we needed to see behind us, we stopped, turned around, and walked back a few steps to still be looking forward. No one asked just how ridiculous our actions were becoming.

Soon a huge land dispute erupted. The once peaceful valley I knew became a verbal war zone. The only visible love I saw was the love vines that grew everywhere choking out weeds and even small trees. The vines of communication between the families that had not been excommunicated were also being pinched off as time progressed.

The land split surely caused a racket. Land, land, and more land talk was all I heard. In the woods discussing land lines The Elder recited Psalms 2: *Why do the heathen rage and the people imagine a vain thing?. . . the rulers take counsel together against the Lord, and against his anointed saying. . . .*

Then he became very upset over dividing the Tennessee land. The surveyor and Abraham, Rudy, and Frank Schrock witnessed The Elder taking off his black felt stovepipe hat and throwing it with a force that smashed it flat when it hit the ground. He began raving and stated. "I hate those Miller children who started all this." He spoke of Delilah, Mattie, and Willie Miller whom he had excommunicated. "Abraham, you know you also owe the other families money for timber. You must pay what God says to avoid a curse."

Abraham stared straight ahead and never uttered a word at that moment.

Land surveyors were called in to survey the colony's 2,000 plus acres of Lael Valley Farms. The Elder decided how many acres to give each family and where to put the stakes and lines. Surveyors explained their procedures based on the curve of the earth and not on straight measurements. The Elder disagreed and ordered the lines be put where he said because it was private land and if the next owner wanted it changed they could.

By not surveying as the professional surveyors said gave Abraham Schrock a few feet less land. The arguments became heated debates to no avail. They were debates between The Elder's demands and what Abraham saw as right because he had put the most money in the land to start with. The Elder refused to speak with Abraham or with the surveyors and sent messages on notes with Uncle David as the messenger boy.

Then Abraham hired a second surveyor without any results, only expenses. Abraham finally gave up the land battle. Once the first surveyor's stakes were in place The Elder ordered the closing of Swanegan Road where Abraham's land ended and Grandpa's began. The Elder ordered huge logs put across the road several thick and rocks piled waist high with a four strand barred wire war fence put up across all the piled stuff.

Abraham Schrock's family received the largest portion of land on the north end of the valley. The rest of the colony families had the south end with our schoolhouse on it. The Elder demanded that the Schrocks use only the north gate to enter and exit their land. The rest of the colony was required to use the east gate.

The Elder ordered, "Nobody in the colony is to go on the Schrock's side of the fence or a curse might be inflicted upon them. There's now a wrong and right side of the fence just like heaven and hell."

Why? What had the Schrocks — all of them — done?

Abraham spoke to his family, "The Elder came with the other fathers to where I was working one day. They talked about dividing the land, and I listened. The Elder interrupted that discussion and said, 'You look terrible with that old hat on your head.' You see! He's trained us men folks to always stop and take off our hats when he comes around in reverence to him — the man of God — outside or anyplace we are. I purposely didn't take my hat off, and I didn't after his remark. He spoke his peace and they called a meeting at the schoolhouse. I went and it lasted into the night. When I left to walk home, I stopped on a bank and stayed there until

130

two o'clock in the morning praying to God for wisdom and guidance."

Abraham paused for a few seconds before continuing. "The answer came clear. It's time for us to move. The Elder says he's dividing up the land here in Lael Valley, and he says that we owe the other families money. Whatever his reasons we will go to Missouri not Mississippi and pick cotton this fall. That will give us money to pay the other families and move."

The Schrock family was given the largest portion of the land. Later that fall, the Schrocks tore down their buildings and took them with them. Then they sold their portion of the land to Champion Paper Company. They were soon gone from the Tennessee valley. Now things were much different in the valley. The Elder began referring to Abraham Schrock, his once right-hand man, as the bull of Bashan, the beast, and the bear. This was hard to imagine. Why all the *veischt* (mean) animals?

The Tennessee land never was ideal for farming. There were too many rocks and hills to grow good crops; it was timberland. The colony people had to go to Mississippi to pick cotton every fall to make a living.

Finally The Elder issued a new decree." The colony is to leave this Tennessee valley and go to the Mississippi Delta to live on a cotton plantation. Each family will leave in the order I give and at the time I say."

The Elder's commands like ocean tides washed in and out. We all struggled to stand as firm as we could until our day came.

The Tennessee valley, our promised land, became a shadow of continual fear. The oak walls enclosed a place of suppressed stress, lost trust, and the death of hope for many colony members.

We were all in a struggle for survival, yet no one would — or could — deal with reality. How many years will we wander through our own wilderness of delusion? Only God knows! Getting into a cult is much easier than getting out.

Chapter 12

Is There Any Hope?

There was so much I didn't understand. But how could I? I was only a child.

Delusion and *confusion* are adult words to describe a psychotic experience. A child settles for "mixed up" and "frightened." I know from personal exposure.

There was no doctor's evaluation. I didn't need one to recognize that my Dad was in bad shape. Things weren't like this in Elkhart. I wish I could talk to him like I did when we came to Lael Valley. His body is here but his mind is someplace else, and I can't reach him. I don't know who he talks to because I can't see any body there. What's going to happen to my dad? What will Mom do? What will happen to Joan, and Fred, and me?

These are questions no six-year-old should have to consider.

My world was bigger than my immediate family. It included colony members and classmates. I liked school, and I liked Aunt Dee, my teacher, but she must be bad. *Is she really going to hell like The Elder said?* I wondered but didn't dare say it out loud. I'm not supposed to talk or think about her, but I miss her. Will I ever like school again? Our new teacher is all right, but will something happen to her too?

What happened to Aunt Dee's brother, Willie, and her sister, Mattie? What did Uncle Willie do that made him so bad? I wish I knew where he went. Aunt Mattie couldn't survive in our oak woods. Is she still alive someplace?

Everything was mixed up. I could tell the grown-ups were upset and didn't want to be bothered by very many questions. So I kept them to myself and wondered. *What will happen to my cousins? Where is Joseph? Did he survive after being dumped? Will I ever be dumped like he was? I believe I'd rather be dead than dumped in a wicked world filled with evil people like he was.*

Life did go on, if you can call it that. We ate. We slept. We worked. There was no joy. Our utopia was gone, and I kept wondering. *Will Luke die from his leg infection? Is he really a bad child? Will he become a woods person living in the hills and wilderness? Could he survive any better than our aunt could? What will happen to him?*

Our warm, accepting family was falling apart. Even The Elder wasn't as popular as he used to be. I couldn't understand how Mary could rebel against The Elder? Isn't she afraid of a curse, going to hell, or getting dumped in the wicked world? And will Susanna ever get over her depression?

I didn't understand why I had so many questions. Fred and Joan didn't seem to be bothered by what was happening. Why me? Mom was doing all she could to take care of Dad and us children.

I finally decided just to make a list of my questions so I wouldn't continually keep asking the same ones.

- Will God punish Joe for playing with dirt and rocks as his trucks?
- Will Freda ever be normal again? Will she ever stop rocking back and forth not talking or eating much?
- What will happen to all the Schrock family?
- Will Aunt Lydia Schrock ever get to visit my Grandma Miller again? I hope so.
- Can all that family survive in the outside world?
- Why does The Elder put members out of the colony into the world when he keeps saying, "None of you are any match for the world."?
- Is Abraham really a *veicht* (mean) bear or bull?
- I know God spared Lovina's life after the poisonous snake bit her. Will she survive the outside world? Maybe God will save her life again in the bad world.

I hope so. I'm glad that God is the final judge. I hope God saves them all and they can come back into Lael Colony and we can all be happy and live together again.

- Will my painful toothaches ever stop?
- Will the puss pockets in my mouth continue to come and burst until all my teeth rot out like some have?
- Is this the persecution and hard times The Elder told us would come?
- Will we have to go in his underground hideout and eat the canned food he had us store in the walls of houses? He keeps quoting Bible passages and says to wait on the Lord.
- Should I teach myself to fast even more in case evil worldly people get me and lock me up?
- Will they likely just kill me because I will say that I have a Bible and believe in God? That's what The Elder predicts.
- Why would I have to die if I was dumped or captured in the outside world? Well, I don't know if I could survive all the evil out there and I might be better off dead before it happens. *God, please help all of us and take the pain away. So many people seem to be hurting here and my tooth hurts now. Please help us all. I will just wait on You, my Lord. I know You, Lord, will take care of us if we obey Your orders from The Elder. Please help! Amen.*
- Why is our promise land getting divided up?
- Why do we have to leave it? I will miss our new home here, our goats, and all the trees – even the acorn Fred planted that is a nice tree now between our goat barn and garden.
- Why are we losing our utopia if God gave it to us?
- Where are we going?
- What will happen to everybody? It's hard to leave behind the only place I know.
- Why won't God allow our gardens and fields to grow well and people to visit each other?

- Why can't everybody get along and be happy as before?
- Is God cursing all of Lael Colony or just the excommunicated ones?
- Will The Elder really come up missing as he indicated and be caught up in the clouds and go to heaven like Elijah did?
- What will happen with him gone?
- The Elder ordered each family to be on their own. Is he training us to be alone without him and not depend on each other any more because we will be scattered in the world and lost?
- Will I be abandoned?
- Will I lose Grandma Miller like I did Grandma Long?
- *Vos iss lets?* (What is wrong?)
- What will happen to my family and relatives and to all the colony members?
- Is there any hope?

My list seemed endless. The future looked bleak. The concept – the idea of an Amish-Jewish colony had been so full of promise. The Elder had seemed so close to God and trustworthy. With the soil so rich and trees so plentiful, why must we move on?

How could intelligent God-fearing people be so duped, so trapped? Is it possible to overcome or rise above anything that happens in life? These situations look and feel impossible. I felt both hopeless and helpless. But even as young as I was, I knew all things are possible with God.

Delusion is costly. Cults always promise so much and return so little. Families are torn apart. Lives are destroyed. I was set on a course to learn the importance of placing more trust in God than in man. God is a solid rock that will stand forever, and man is fallible.

This book, *Delusion*, is the first in a series and only opens the door to the main story. The next book, *Deception*, will disclose the extent of error that occurs within a cult and the impact it has on families. *Deliverance*, the final book in the series, will share the unfolding of God's grace. It will reveal His deliverance from bondage and misguided adherence to cultish demands to a place of freedom in Him and in society.

Patricia Hochstetler

Epilogue

Dear Reader,

Few people ever intend to become a part of a cult. By its very nature a cult implies a degree of submission to someone highly revered or even worshipped.

The group may be called a sect, a gang, a colony, or a compound. When authority is held by only one person, when all decisions are made by one individual, or when the right to make personal choices is in jeopardy, there is a danger of becoming cultish.

No child can ever be held responsible for becoming a part of a cult. Growing up in a colony similar to if not actually a cult offers limited opportunity to learn about choices and options. Though not by the child's choice, the colony – the cult – is its world. Young children are caught up in cults and gangs. Only adults make the decision to become members of a colony or cult.

As a small child, I had nothing to say about moving or going into our colony. Much like a caged bird, I knew nothing of the outside world. Growing up in the colony seemed normal, and I believed in the only thing I knew. I tried to abide by all the rules and laws and be perfect as expected.

I felt good about struggling to do right and being different from the worldly people who I understood were all heathens going to hell. I had a chance to go to heaven if I did what our leader and my parents told me to do. What a privilege! That made me happy in the Lord and content to be where I lived. Not knowing a thing concerning colonies, religion, or brainwashing, I remained puppet-like and willing to suffer in any way – or lose my life – for what I felt was God's cause.

I knew this historical story must be told to glorify God, my Deliverer, and for family history. Being the first to speak out publicly about this 60-year-old, secret, religious colony seemed scary but a "must" to honor God. Plunging forward with inspiration, I felt determined to use my past experience as stepping-stones to the future.

I've shared my heart and feelings giving you a slice of my childhood as I recall it and as told through other Lael Colony members. Some happenings are omitted, and some names are changed by request. I would not knowingly hurt anyone. I wrote this book to give others hope of overcoming obstacles in their lives and to caution those who may be considering joining a secretive group or gang dominated by one or a very select few.

This book, *Delusion*, shows God's protection and the results of His matchless power. My prayer is that others will benefit from my experiences and see the dangers in any brainwashing, cult-like atmosphere before they decide if a group is really what they want. For those who find themselves in similar circumstances, I have written this account of my experiences to provide a ray of hope that you, too, can be set free. My dream is that people will always trust our infallible God more than man who is fallible.

At the end of this book, *Delusion,* it is 1954, and I am six years old. The second book in the series, *Deception,* covers the next 10 years and deals with a colony move, death, law enforcement, more rules, and brainwashing. In the third book of this series, *Deliverance,* I am sixteen and it is 1964. I am delivered from the cult and cast into a foreign world to face the horrors caused by being a caged child. It is my story of learning to deal with culture shock right here in the United States. It is a declaration of God's protection and deliverance.